Better Homes and Gardens®

FAMILY ROOM PROJECTS
YOU CAN BUILD

BETTER HOMES AND GARDENS BOOKS

Editorial Director: Don Dooley
Executive Editor: Gerald M. Knox
Art Director: Ernest Shelton   Asst. Art Director: Randall Yontz
Production and Copy Editor: David Kirchner
Building and Remodeling Editor: Noel Seney
Building Books Editor: Larry Clayton
Contributing Architectural Editor: Stephen Mead
Remodeling and Home Maintenance Editor: David R. Haupert
Building Ideas Editor: Douglas M. Lidster
Remodeling Ideas Editor: Dan Kaercher
Kitchens, Appliances, Home Management Editor: Joan McCloskey
Associate Editors: Kristelle Petersen, Cheryl Scott
Graphic Designers: Harijs Priekulis, Faith Berven, Sheryl Veenschoten, Rich Lewis

CONTENTS

A-PLACE-FOR-
EVERYTHING
PROJECTS

Busy places like family rooms have an affinity for accumulating the family belongings. Games, books, magazines, puzzles, hobby materials, entertainment equipment, and varied collectibles always find their way to the family gathering space.

That's fine, but most family rooms would still benefit if all these miscellaneous items had a special place to call their own.

All the projects in this chapter work toward that goal—they help you organize the family room. And these designs are especially adaptable to your family's changing interests and possessions.

The location you choose for your project can also make a big difference in the appearance of the family room. Wall-hung units save valuable floor space and add interest to a plain wall, and room dividers help to organize and create new usable space.

But whatever projects you choose, the time, effort, skills, and materials you invest will all pay off in convenience and good looks for a long time to come.

ROOM DIVIDER PLUS STORAGE

Put this easy-to-build book-shelf wherever you need help dividing space. It does that job neatly, and as a bonus, it provides convenient storage for stereo components, records, and large-sized books.

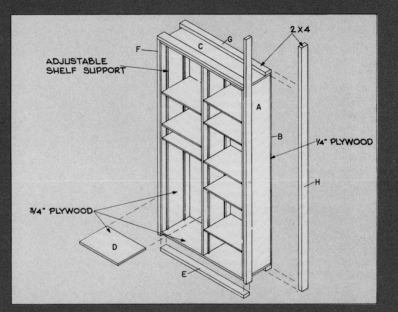

1 Cut the surround (A and C) and shelves (D) from ¾-inch plywood. To make the edges of the shelves fit flush against the verticals, cut grooves in the verticals deep and wide enough to accept the shelf support strips. (Or notch the ends of each shelf to fit around the strips.) Fasten the strips to the verticals 12 inches apart.

2 Position the five pieces on the floor and assemble with butt joints, using glue and finishing nails.

3 Glue and nail the plywood back (B) to each of the verticals and top and bottom.

4 Apply veneer tape to all plywood edges on the front of the unit (see page 85).

5 Cut 2x4s (E,F,G,H) to length. Notch F to fit over baseboard molding. Cut H about ¼ inch less than floor-to-ceiling height.

6 Sand and stain all 2x4s.

7 Fasten E,F,G to unit with screws from the inside. Position unit in room and attach outer 2x4 uprights (H).

8 Seal and paint all of the plywood. Varnish 2x4s.

Materials (for a 51x96x16¼-in. divider):

¾-in. plywood—2 shts.
  A 3 16x72 in.
  C 2 16x48 in.
  D 9 16x22⅞ in.

¼-in. plywood—1 sht.
  B 1 48x73½ in.

2x4 pine or fir—60 ft.
  E 2 48 in.   G 2 49½ in.
  F 2 75 in.   H 2 96 in.

Glue, nails, shelf supports, wood filler, stain, varnish, sealer, and paint.

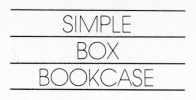

SIMPLE BOX BOOKCASE

This natural-finish bookcase makes a fast project for an inexperienced furniture builder. It's simply two boxes screwed to end panels. The space between the boxes is a convenient storage bonus for magazines. Choose good-looking hardwood for this project if you want to leave the wood exposed. Or use fir or pine if you plan to paint the unit.

1 Cut all 1x12 pieces to the length specified in the materials list. To assemble the two rectangular boxes, use butt joints (see page 75). Long horizontal pieces (C) should be flush with outside face of shorter end pieces (D). Fasten with glue and nails.

2 Insert the backs (A), making sure that they're flush with the edges of the box. Glue and nail from outside.

3 Rest the lower box on two bricks (or other objects) to raise it off the floor. Screw the end panels (B) into place; countersink the screws.

4 Turn bookcase upside down and repeat step 3 to anchor top box in place.

5 Sand smooth. Stain and seal with varnish.

Materials (for a 40½x43½x11½-in. bookcase):

1x12—34 ft.
- A 2 40½ in.
- B 2 40½ in.
- C 4 42 in.
- D 4 11½ in.

Flathead screws, glue, stain, nails, and varnish.

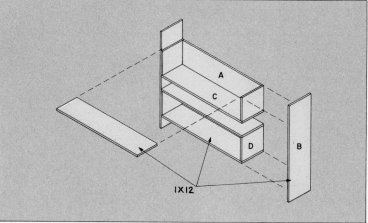

TURN-A-CORNER SHELVING

If every inch of shelving is accounted for at your house, use the walls of your family room for additional stashing space. Narrow, floor-to-ceiling shelving will fit in even the smallest room to hold your library or collectibles in fine style. You'll need to give up less than a running foot of floor space to incorporate this shelving system in your home.

1 Dado verticals (A) to accommodate shelf supports.

2 At corner, attach one vertical (A) to wall and nail another to it at a right angle for left shelf section. Use metal angle on front vertical to attach it to wall at ceiling.

3 Position remaining four verticals to divide wall into quarters. Fasten to wall at ceiling with angles. Apply facings (E), centering on verticals.

4 Nail sleepers (F,G) to floor. Nail bottom shelves (B,C) to sleepers (F,G). Nail bottom facing (D,H) to sleepers and shelf edge, flush with facing (E) on verticals.

5 Apply facing strips (D,H) to remaining shelves (B,C) fitting flush with shelf tops and allowing space at ends to align with vertical trim (E).

6 Attach shelf supports to verticals (A). Insert clips.

7 Nail the remaining facing material (I) to fit over the verticals at the ceiling.

8 Sand. Paint unit and shelves. Install shelves when dry.

Materials (96x93¼x10¼-in.) unit —one wall and corner only):

1x10 pine or fir—82 ft.
  A 6 96 in.
  B 12 20 in.
  C 4 29½ in.

1x2 pine or fir—88 ft.
  D 12 19¼ in.   E 5 94½ in.
  H 4 18⅞ in.   I 1 82¼ in.

1x1 pine or fir—22 ft.
  F 2 29½ in.
  G 6 20 in.

Metal angle braces, glue, screws, nails, adjustable shelf supports, and paint.

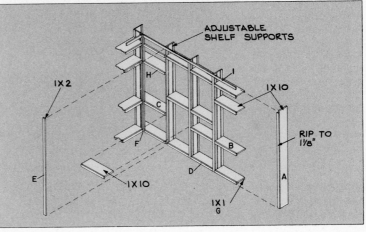

'ROUND AND 'ROUND SHELVING

If support columns interrupt your basement family room, capitalize on the intrusion. Enclose them, add some shelves, and let them work for you. If you like, build a platform for seating like the one shown here and decorate it with splashy colors to further define the living area of the room.

1 Frame the posts with 2x4s (A,B,C).

2 Cut plasterboard to size (D,E) and apply to framing. Nail metal corner bead on corners.

3 Finish corners using metal corner bead and premixed joint compound. Paint plasterboard.

4 Using mitered joints (see page 77), apply quarter round (F,G) where the plasterboard meets the ceiling.

5 Screw adjustable shelf supports through plasterboard into 2x4s. Mount strips equidistant from floor to ceiling.

6 Measure width and depth of enclosure and transfer measurements to plywood for shelves (H). (The rectangle should be large enough to allow a 6-inch shelf along one side and a 12-inch shelf along the other.) Cut out sections with saber saw.

7 Sand and paint shelves. Install. If desired, build the raised platform from 2x6s topped with plywood, making cutouts to accommodate shelves.

Materials (90x36x28-in. unit):

2x4 pine or fir—96 ft.
  A 4 13¾ in.
  B 4 22 in.
  C 10 87 in.
½-in. plasterboard—2 shts.
  D 2 30x90 in.
  E 2 13¾x90 in.
½x½-in. quarter round—10 ft.
  F 2 16 in.   G 2 31 in.
½-in. plywood—1½ shts.
  H 4 28x36 in.
Metal corner bead, joint compound, shelf brackets, adjustable shelf supports, screws, nails, and paint.

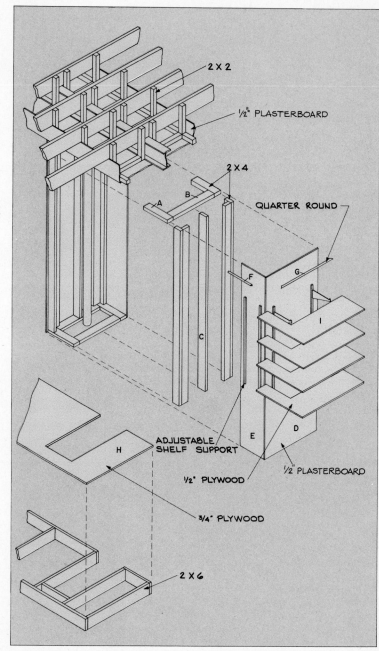

HANDY DESK TOP CATCHALL

If you're one of those people who can never seem to find your car keys, pens, pencils, or the power or water bill, this is your lucky day. With this ever-ready organizer around, desk clutter needn't be a problem. Build the unit to fit on top of your desk and customize the openings to fit your particular set of circumstances.

1 Cut the three 1x6 verticals (A) to length. Miter (see page 77) the ends of two of the verticals. Be sure to choose a top grade of pine for the best finished appearance.

2 Cut the shelves (C) and the four dividers (D). Glue and nail the dividers to one shelf. Butt-join (see page 75) the shelves to the verticals using glue and nails. Countersink the finishing nails so they won't show when you paint unit.

3 Cut the top shelf (B); miter both of the ends. Glue and nail the shelf in place.

4 Cut the plywood back (E) in an ''L'' shape. Glue and nail it in position as shown in sketch.

5 Fill all of the exposed nail holes; sand smooth and give the organizer a finish coat of varnish.

Materials (for an 18x28x6-in. unit):

1x6 pine—12 ft.
   A 3 18 in.
   B 1 14⅜ in.
   C 3 12⅞ in.
   D 4 5 in.
¼-in. plywood—½ sht.
   E 1 17⅝x27¼ in.
Nails, glue, wood filler, and varnish or polyurethane.

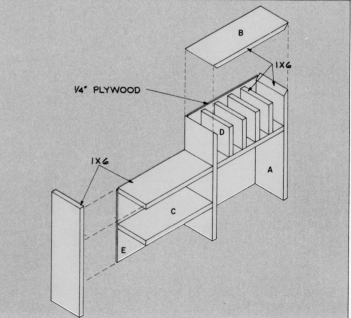

OPEN BOX WALL STORAGE

This artful arrangement of open boxes dresses up a wall and gives you storage in the bargain. Vary the individual box sizes to fit your storables and add shelves where you can use them.

1 Butt-join (see page 75) box sides and back with glue and nails. Install shelves, if desired, by nailing through from outside of boxes.

2 Fill nail holes and exposed edges with wood filler, and sand. Paint or stain. Fasten to wall with toggle bolts (see page 84).

Materials (for project shown):

½-in. plywood—2½ shts.

A 2 12x18x4-in. boxes
    4 4x11 in.   2 11x17 in.
    4 4x18 in.

B 2 12x18x6-in. boxes
    4 6x17 in.   2 11x17 in.
    4 6x12 in.

C 1 12x12x12-in. box
    2 11x12 in.   1 11x11 in.
    2 12x12 in.

D 2 12x18x9-in. boxes
    4 9x17 in.   2 11x17 in.
    4 9x12 in.

E 1 12x12x4-in. box
    2 4x11 in.   1 11x11 in.
    2 4x12 in.

F 1 12x12x15-in. box
    2 11x15 in.   1 11x11 in.
    2 12x15 in.

G 2 12x18x12-in. boxes
    4 12x17 in.   2 11x17 in.
    4 12x12 in.

H 1 6x18x12-in. box
    2 6x11 in.   1 11x17 in.
    2 6x18 in.

Nails, screws, glue, edging tape or wood filler, and paint or stain.

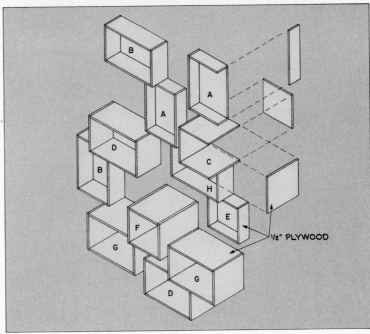

½" PLYWOOD

SLIDE IN-SLIDE OUT SHELVING

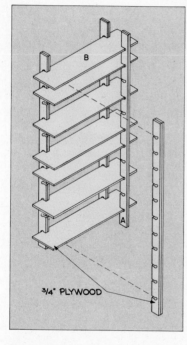

3/4" PLYWOOD

This floor-to-ceiling shelf system is super simple to build. It's mostly a matter of cutting a few notches and slipping the whole unit together. You can easily adjust the overall size of the unit, too, if your family room requires more storage space.

1 Cut verticals (A) from plywood. They should all be 4 inches wide. You'll need a total of eight plywood strips each 8 feet long (or longer if your ceiling is over standard height). If you adjust the overall width, plan to have additional uprights every 4 feet. If you plan to use this unit against a wall, notch out the necessary space for the baseboard molding on the verticals with a coping saw.

2 Laminate two strips of plywood together using white glue and clamps to make four verticals in all. Allow adhesive to dry thoroughly before proceeding. (If you prefer an easier route, use 2x4s for verticals and 1x12s for shelves to eliminate the lamination and the extra cutting.)

3 Drill 1-inch-diameter holes centered 1½ inches in from edge of each vertical. Holes should be 12 inches apart. Cut a ¾-inch notch from edge through to hole.

4 Position verticals between floor and ceiling. They should be set 8 inches apart with a 36-inch span. Fasten verticals with metal angles.

5 Cut shelves 4 feet long and 1 foot wide (B). Slip shelves through notches in verticals leaving about a 6-inch overhang on each end.

6 Sand and finish unit with two coats of urethane.

Materials (for a 48x96x14-in. shelf system):

¾-in. plywood—2 shts.
  A 8 4x96 in.
  B 7 12x48 in.

Metal angles, white glue, and urethane.

PIGEONHOLE BAR AND BOOKCASE

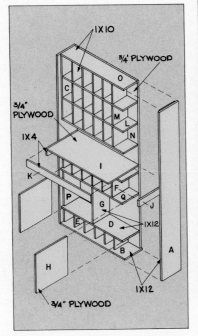

This great-looking compartmentalized bar is reminiscent of old office mail sorters. It's a snap to keep things tidy because the cubbyholes make a place for everything.

1 For top pigeonhole section (C,O,L,M), cut ⅜x¾-inch dadoes in sides (C) to accept shelves (L). Cut ¼x¾-inch dadoes in shelves (O,L) to accept dividers (M). Assemble with glue and nails.

2 For bottom pigeonhole and cabinet unit (P,Q,F,G,D), cut ¼x¾-inch dadoes in top and middle shelves (D,Q) to receive dividers (F). Dado bottom (D) and middle shelf (Q) to receive divider (G). Dado sides (P) to receive middle shelf (Q). Assemble bottom cubbyhole and cabinet section using glue and nails.

3 Cut out pieces for bar top (I,J,K). Miter corners of edge trim (J,K) and assemble using glue and nails.

4 Butt-join bottom dividers (E) to base (B), and glue and nail to back (N).

5 Glue and nail assembled bottom pigeonhole and cabinet unit to back (N), then add top pigeonhole unit.

6 Stand upright and add bar top and sides (A).

7 Install the doors (H) and add magnetic catches.

8 Fill all plywood edges with wood putty. Sand the entire unit and paint.

Materials (84x37½-in. unit):

¾-in. plywood—3 shts.

C	2	10x30 in.	P	2 11x30¾ in.
O	2	10x36 in.	Q	1 11x35¼ in.
L	2	10x35¼ in.	F	5 11x10½ in.
M	15	10x10½ in.	G	1 11x20½ in.
I	1	34½x20½ in.	D	2 11x36 in.
A	2	12x84 in.	H	2 18x21½ in.
B	1	12x36 in.	E	7 11x10 in.

1x3 pine or fir—8 ft.

J 2 22 in.

K 2 36 in.

¼-inch plywood—1 sht.

N 1 36x83¼ in.

Hinges, catches, plastic laminate, and adhesive, glue, nails, and paint.

VERSATILE ADJUSTABLE SHELVES

This unique storage wall hides some real surprises. It's easy to build, and it's adjustable, too.

Once the frame is built, you can add and subtract shelves in fast fashion whenever you want.

1 Sandwich each pair of uprights (B) between a series of 16-inch-long 1x4s (C) (don't attach the bottom pairs). Space them 1 inch apart, keeping front and back edges flush. Use glue and nails to secure.

2 Nail stretchers (A) between the bottom pairs of 1x4s to form a box with the front stretcher set back 3 inches.

3 Glue and nail the assembled sides to the boxes.

4 Cut plywood top (D) to size and nail it to the assembled sides, making sure top and bottom of sides are equally spaced.

5 Stand unit upright and place in position. Slide bottom shelves (E) in place.

6 Cut a ¼-inch-deep dado (see page 76) in top of one shelf (E) and bottom of another to receive hardboard vertical dividers (L). Install dividers; glue if desired.

7 Apply plastic bypassing door track on top and bottom of two shelves. Slip sliding doors (M) into tracks.

8 Screw a piano hinge to edge of shelves for closable sections. Screw doors (J,K) to piano hinges on shelf. (See page 82.) Use chain stops on door (K) to hold shelf level.

9 Assemble drawers (F,G,H,I) (see page 81). Bottom of drawer (F) will extend ¾ inch beyond each side of drawer (G). Slip

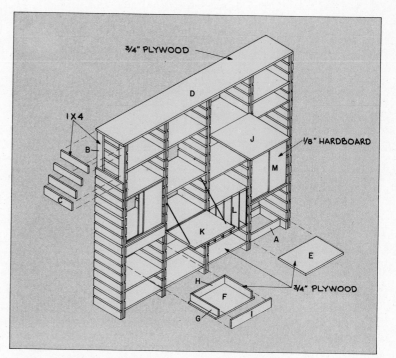

drawers into slots formed by sandwich on verticals.

10 Sand and paint the unit.

Materials (for an 85¼x96x16-in.-deep unit):

¾-in. plywood—2½ shts.

D	1	16x96 in.
E	20	16x22⅝ in.
F	3	16x22⅝ in.
G	6	3¾x16 in.
H	3	3¾x19⅝ in.
I	3	4½x22⅝ in.
J	1	22½x22⅝ in.
K	1	17x22⅝ in.

1x4 pine or fir—350 ft.

A	8	21⅛ in.	C	190	16 in.
B	10	84½ in.			

⅛-in. hardboard—1 sht.

L	6	17¾x16 in.
M	4	11x21¼ in.

Piano hinges, chain stops, bypassing door tracks, nails, glue, and paint.

STACKING STORAGE SYSTEM

These stackable boxes make a modular storage center that fits almost anywhere. There are just three basic pieces; the closed boxes are repeated seven times for lots of hidden storage. The boxes are based on 28-inch-square modules. Only the depths of the units vary. If you adjust sizes, make sure they remain square so you can rearrange them easily.

1 Plan your boxes to fit along a family room wall. Adjust sizes as necessary.

2 For the smaller open box, butt-join (see page 75) frame (F,G) using glue and nails. Attach flush back (H); insert shelf (G) and nail from outside.

3 For the larger open box, follow the same procedure with pieces (I,J,L). Add vertical dividers (K) as shown.

4 Assemble sides (A), top and bottom (B), and shelf (C) following the same procedure. Attach recessed back (D). Install the flush door with hinges (see page 82). Add magnetic catch, as in photo at upper corner.

5 Fill plywood edges with wood filler or apply veneer tape. Countersink nails, fill all nail holes, and sand and paint each unit. If you wish, you can add extra interest to the units by painting on colorful graphics.

Materials (for one 28x28x8-in. open unit, one 28x56x8-in. open unit, and one 28x28x16-in. closed unit):

¾-in. plywood—1½ shts.
    A 2 15¼x28 in.

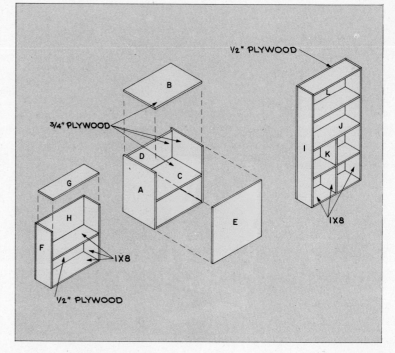

B 2 15¼x26½ in.
C 1 14½x26½ in.
D 1 26½x26½ in.
E 1 28x28 in.
½-in. plywood—1 sht.
  H 1 28x28 in. L 1 56x28 in.

1x8 pine or fir—42 ft.
  F 2 28 in.   G,J 8 26½ in.
  I 2 56 in.   K 2 13¹⁄₁₆ in.
Pivot hinges, magnetic catch, edging tape or wood filler, glue, nails, and paint.

18

FLIP-TOP STORAGE BOX

This tailored little chest gives you extra storage and comfortable seating all in one sturdy unit. And, the inside is divided to keep your storables well-organized.

1 Assemble chest sides (A), front and back (F), and bottom (B) using butt joints (see page 75), glue, and finishing nails.

2 Glue and nail the plywood divider strips (G) to the front and back panels (F).

3 Nail the hinging strip (C) to the top of back and side panels. Screw piano hinge to ¾-inch face of the strip.

4 Align top (D) with hinge and strip (C); screw top to hinge.

5 Glue and nail the front lip of top (E) in place.

6 Assemble the interior boxes that sit on dividers. Butt-join sides (H,I) with glue and nails. Inset ¼-inch plywood bottom (J) flush with bottom of box using glue and nails. Install the dividers (K) flush with top of box; glue and nail.

7 Countersink nails, fill all nail holes, and sand, seal, and paint outside of chest. Sand interior boxes smooth and finish with two coats of polyurethane.

Materials (24x36x12-in. chest):

¾-in. plywood—2 shts.
- A 2 11¼x24 in.
- B 1 24x34½ in.
- C,E 2 4x36 in.
- D 1 20x36 in.
- F 2 34½x10½ in.
- G 3 6½x22½ in.
- H 4 4x10 in.
- I 4 4x15¾ in.
- K 4 3¾x8½ in.

¼-in. plywood—¼ sht.
- J 2 8½x15¾ in.

1x2 pine—4 ft.
- L 2 22½ in.

Piano hinge, screws, nails, glue, paint, and polyurethane.

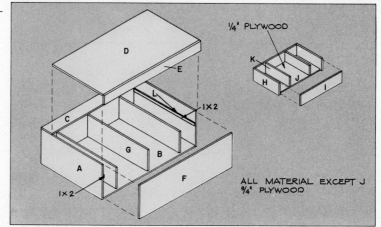

ALL MATERIAL EXCEPT J ¾" PLYWOOD

18

STURDY SHELF AND BOOKRACK

This handsome bookcase is easily built—and easily adapted to suit your individual needs. If you like, make it as tall as a wall simply by cutting the vertical supports to the desired height and adding the appropriate number of shelves.

1 Cut out all pieces taking best advantage of the wood grain lines on all vertical and horizontal members.

2 Following the sketch, drill pairs of ¾-inch-diameter holes in the verticals (A) to a depth of ¼ inch. Space pairs 10½ inches apart. Center a pilot hole for screws in each hole, drilling completely through the verticals and into the 2x12 shelves (B).

3 Position the shelves. Glue and screw legs to the shelves using flathead screws.

4 Cut ¾-inch-diameter dowel in ¼-inch lengths to plug the screw holes.

5 Cut the end blocks (C,D) to fit flush with the face of the verticals and snug with the shelf tops and bottoms, Screw to sides of verticals.

6 Sand and finish unit with two coats of polyurethane.

NOTE: If you'd like to paint the bookshelves, use fir or pine dimension lumber. Follow general directions for assembly, but use countersunk nails instead of screws. Fill nail holes, sand all edges smooth, and paint as desired.

Materials (for a 48x42-in. bookcase):

1x4 oak—16 ft.
  A 4 42 in.
2x12 oak—16 ft.
  B 4 48 in.
¾-inch plywood—½ sht.
  C 6 9x13 in.
  D 2 6x13 in.
Glue, screws, ¾-inch dowel, nails, and polyurethane.

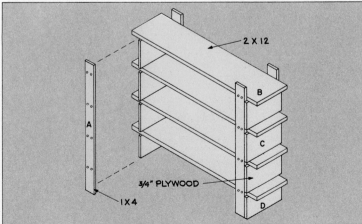

2 X 12

B

A

C

¾" PLYWOOD

1 X 4

D

MULTI-FUNCTION MARVELS

Anytime you can get one project to perform more than one job, you're money and space ahead . . . and each of these projects is designed to do just that. Whether it's more seating, another table surface, or extra work space you need, you'll find a project here to fill the bill, with built–in storage, to boot.

Start by considering what you need most. If it's more table space, determine where it will serve you best. The tables you'll find here all store flat against the wall to free valuable floor space when they're not in use. And, if it's seating you're short of, put the dead space in a spare corner to use. Our solution turns a corner of a room into a multi-level, multi-function seating and play space.

Any of these ideas is easily adapted to your own particular room just by changing the dimensions in the materials list. And if your carpentry skills are a bit rusty, there's a section of building basics in the back of the book to help you out.

So why wait. Choose your pet project and get started!

LOW-LINE SEATING MODULE

These sturdy modules fill two needs—besides making for attractive seating, they also provide functional display storage. You'll find them quite simple to build, too. They go together so quickly that you'll be able to assemble several to use around the fireplace tonight.

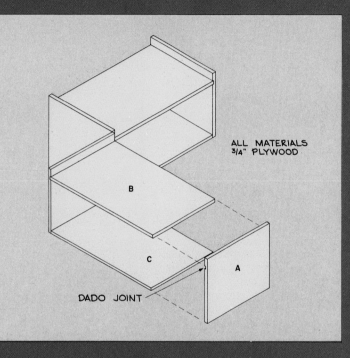

ALL MATERIALS 3/4" PLYWOOD

DADO JOINT

1 Dado end panels (A) 2 inches down from top edge to receive seat base (B). Since these modules are built without backs, dado shelf construction (see page 76) on the seat gives the unit extra strength. If you plan to use the modules for storage, rather than seating, use butt joints (see page 75).

2 Run a bead of glue in dado joint and slip seat base in position. Nail through from the face of the end panel with finishing nails to hold seat securely in place.

3 Butt-join bottom of unit (C) and end panels (A) with glue and nails. Bottom should be flush with bottom edge of end panels. Using corner clamps during construction will speed your work and help you achieve more accurate joints. Be sure to countersink all of the nails at this point.

4 Fill and sand all exposed plywood edges and nail holes. Paint as desired.

5 If you wish, add a piece of foam pad, covered with fabric that complements your decor, to cushion the seating area.

Materials (for one 18x30x16-in. module):

¾-in. plywood—½ sht.
   A 2 16x18 in.
   B 1 18x29¼ in.
   C 1 18x28½ in.
Glue, wood filler, nails, and paint or varnish.

When you need a wall of storage and another table, yet you don't want to give up much floor space, here's the answer. Shelves running from floor to ceiling hold a host of family room necessities, while the table folds up when not in service, freeing up valuable floor space for other activities.

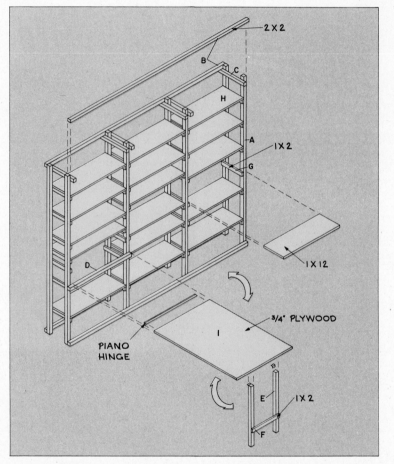

1 Cut all verticals (A) and top and bottom horizontals (B) from 2x2s. Cut all shelf supports (G) from 1x2s. Sandwich a pair of 2x2 verticals (A) between 1x2s (G), spacing 1x2s according to desired shelf locations for two interior uprights. Nail single 1x2s (G) on insides of outer posts for shelf supports.

2 Cut hortizontals (B). Drill holes through bottom of verticals (A) and horizontals (B). Butt-join (see page 75) with carriage bolts.

3 Cut and attach top horizontals (C) 1½ inches down from top of each vertical (A). Drill and bolt together as in sketch.

4 Attach top rail (B) to uprights (rail will rest on 2x2s (C)). Drill and bolt as before.

5 Cut shelves (H) from 1x12 material to fit between verticals (A) and to rest on 1x2s (G). Nail shelves in place.

6 Cut ledger (D) and bolt to face of two verticals, 28 inches from floor, for table surface. Cut table surface (I) from plywood. Surface should be the same width as the distance between two verticals.

7 Make table legs from 2x2s (E) with a 1x2 stretcher (F). Legs should be cut to same height as top of 2x2 (D). Attach legs to top using loose pin butt hinges. Attach a piano hinge to 2x2 ledger (D) and to tabletop (I).

8 Finish tabletop with plastic laminate. Apply two coats of clear sealer to wood. Add cabinet catch to keep tabletop in upright position when not in use. If you wish, use metal angles on the legs and continual angle brace to attach tabletop to horizontal (D) for a stationary working surface.

Materials (84x102x11½-in. storage wall with 32x48-in. tabletop):

2x2 cedar, pine, or fir—120 ft.

A	8 84 in.	D	1 35 in.
B	4 102 in.	E	2 28 in.
C	6 14½ in.		

1x2 cedar, pine, or fir—40 ft.

F	1 16 in.	G	38 11½ in.

1x12 cedar, pine, or fir—48 ft.

H 17 32 in.

¾-in. plywood—½ sht.

I 1 32x48 in.

Piano hinge, butt hinges, plastic laminate, contact cement, nails, carriage bolts, cabinet catch, glue, and clear sealer.

WRAP-AROUND STORAGE SEAT

This L-shaped seating and storage unit turns an empty corner into a big plus in any family room. The top is spacious enough for comfortable seating or lounging. Add a comfy cushion atop, if you like. And, there's room enough to tuck plenty of play equipment behind the sliding doors.

1 Cut and construct the base of the unit of 1x3s (J,K,L,M,N). Miter (see page 77) projecting corners and butt-join (see page 76) other corners. Nail the base to the wall.
2 Cut the plywood bottom (I) to fit on top of base with a 2-inch overhang at front and one end. Nail to the base.
3 Cut end panels (Q) and verticals (E,F) from plywood, and uprights (G,H) and ledgers (B,C,D) from dimension lumber. Notch dividers (E,F) to receive 1x2 ledger (B). Position the dividers (E,F) and uprights (G,H,Q) by toenailing them to the bottom and wall as needed. Assemble ledger (B,C,D) and fasten to wall and uprights.
4 Cut door track for ¾-inch-thick doors to fit between the vertical panels. Each section requires a piece of bypassing track at top and bottom. Screw track to the bottom.
5 Cut seat (A) from plywood. Seat should overhang the verticals by ¾ inch. Attach the seat to verticals and ledger using glue and finishing nails. Screw track for sliding doors to underside of seat.
6 Cut doors (O,P) from plywood and mount in tracks. Add recessed finger pulls or drill a ¾-inch hole through doors.

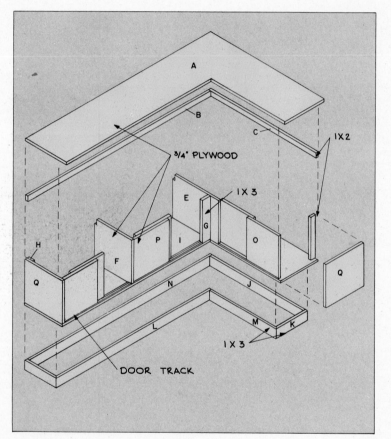

7 Paint the unit and cover seat with plastic laminate.

Materials (for a 60x36¾-in. seating/storage bench):

¾-in. plywood—2 shts.
  A 1 36¾x60 in. (cut to L shape 12¾ in. wide)
  E 1 12x14½ in.   F 1 12x12 in.
  I 1 60x36 in. (cut to L-shape 12 in. wide)
  O 2 11x12 in.   Q 2 12x12 in.
  P 4 12x12 in.

1x2 pine or fir—12 ft.
  B 1 57¾ in.
  C 1 34½ in.
  H 2 12 in.

1x3 pine or fir—18 ft.
  G 1 12 in.
  J 1 32½ in.
  N 1 59¼ in.
  K 2 10 in.
  L 1 50¾ in.
  M 1 24 in.

Bypassing door track, plastic laminate and adhesive, glue, nails, and paint.

MULTI-LEVEL ENVIRONMENT

It takes an ambitious craftsman to tackle this project, but the fruit of the labor is worth it. You'll get seating, storage, and recreation space in one corner.

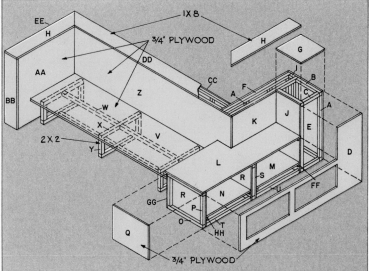

1 Butt-join (see page 75) framework for wrap/around wall using 2x2s for posts (A) and top and bottom braces (B,C,I,F,CC). Nail to floor and side wall.

2 Apply skins (E,J,K,Z,AA,BB, EE). Nail and glue to framing.

3 Miter joints (see page 77) of cap (H,DD) and nail to framing. Butt cap (G) against cap (H); nail.

4 Build storage box using 2x2 framing; nail bottom and top braces (O) and posts (P) together using butt joints. Glue and nail sides (R,S) to framing. Separate with bottom braces (T,U) and glue and nail together.

5 Nail the ledgers (FF,HH) to sides and to skin (J). Insert the shelves (M,N) on ledgers.

6 Cut openings in facing (D). Glue and nail facing (D), side (Q), top (L), and side (GG) to framing. Set in place.

7 Butt-join, glue, and nail posts (Y) and top and bottom braces (X). Glue and nail top and bottom stretchers (W) between braces.

8 Glue and nail sofa seat (V) in place. Fill all exposed plywood edges and paint entire unit.

Materials (for project shown):

¾-in. plywood—7 shts.

D	1	35¼x74 in.	V	1 26x87½ in.
E	1	21x35¼ in.	Z	2 35¼x96 in.
G	1	15x14¼ in.		
J	1	14¼x35¼ in.		
K	1	26¼x35¼ in.		
L	1	22¾x59 in.		
M	1	13½x26¼ in.		
N	1	21¼x26¾ in.		
Q	1	18x22 in.		
R	2	18x21¼ in.		
S	1	13½x18 in.		
AA	2	34½x35¼ in.		
BB	1	7½x35¼ in.		
EE	1	35¼x40½ in.		
GG	1	18x31¼ in.		

1x8 pine or fir—18 ft.

H	2	42 in.	DD	1 103½ in.

2x2 pine or fir—210 ft.

A	26	32¼ in.	P	4 15 in.
B	4	14¼ in.	T	2 26¾ in.
C	2	10½ in.	U	2 26¼ in.
F	8	40½ in.	W	4 38 in.
I	16	3 in.	X	6 23 in.
O	4	21¼ in.	Y	6 8¼ in.
CC	4	89¼ in.		

1x1 pine or fir—6 ft.

FF	3	13½ in.	HH	2 21¼ in.

Glue, wood filler, paint.

THREE-PART WORK CENTER

Room for an extra table is usually hard to find. That's why this fold-down table makes a lot of sense in any family room. When it's not in use as a hobby or game table, it folds flat against the wall. Two other simply constructed units create storage space and an additional working counter.

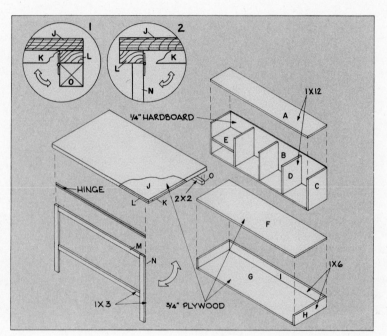

For table:

1 Cut ledger (O) to length. Locate wall studs and fasten ledger to wall with wood screws so top of ledger is 33 inches from floor.
2 Cut tabletop (J) from ¾-inch plywood. Cut edging strips (K,L) and attach to edges of tabletop with glue and finishing nails. Cover tabletop with plastic laminate, if desired.
3 Attach tabletop to ledger (O) using a piano hinge, as shown in inset 1. Tabletop should extend 5 inches beyond each end of (O).
4 Cut legs (N) and stretchers (M). Assemble leg support unit using metal angle braces.
5 Center leg unit on bottom of tabletop so legs are 2 inches from each end, and attach piano hinge as shown in inset 2. Make sure legs clear the ends of ledger (O) when they are folded up.

For upper storage unit:

1 Cut the top and the bottom (A) and the side panels (C) from 1x12s. Assemble using butt joints (see page 75).
2 Cut the ¼-inch hardboard back (B) to fit ¼ inch in from the edges of the box. Attach with glue and headed brads.
3 Cut the dividers (D) and the small shelf (E) from 1x12s. Mark spacing and install with butt joints.

For shelf/surface unit:

1 Cut bottom (G) from plywood. Cut 1x6s (H,I), and glue and nail to bottom (G) using butt joints.
2 Attach assembled part of unit (G,H,I) to wall studs with wood screws. Support underneath with metal angle braces.

3 Cut top (F) from plywood to fit flush with edges of 1x6s; glue and nail in place.
4 Surface top and edges with plastic laminate. Paint all units as desired.

Materials (for a 36x60-in. table):

¾-in. plywood—1 sht.
  J 1 36x60 in.
1x2 pine or fir—12 ft.
  K 2 33 in.
  L 1 60 in.
1x3 pine or fir—16 ft.
  M 2 51 in.
  N 2 33 in.
2x2 pine or fir—6 ft.
  O 1 50 in.

For upper storage unit (16x60-in.):
1x12 pine or fir—20 ft.
  A 2 58½ in. C 2 16 in.
  D 3 14½ in.
  E 1 14½ in.
¼-in. hardboard—1 sht.
  B 1 15½x59½ in.
For shelf/surface unit (20x60 in.):
¾-in. plywood—1 sht.
  F 1 20x60 in.
  G 1 58½x19¼ in.
1x6 pine or fir—10 ft.
  H 2 20 in.
  I 1 58½ in.
Plastic laminate, contact cement, two piano hinges, metal angle braces, headed brads, glue, nails, screws, and paint.

HOBBY/ WORK CENTERS

Every family member has some special interest that takes up space. But in order to really enjoy a hobby, you need plenty of room to spread it out. And the last thing you want to do is pack it all up after every go-round.

The projects in this chapter were chosen to help you organize your hobby area to happily integrate your interests with the rest of the family activities. Even if you think you don't have room for everyone's hobbies, there's a project here for converting any unused corner into a convenient work space.

Any of these designs is flexible enough to be used by one or more family members even with their varied interests. A large working surface can become an area for pattern cutting, model building, or whatever. And extra storage helps keep all the necessary hobby gear close at hand.

Once you've found the project and the place to locate it, the rest is easy. Brush up on your building basics with the section at the back of the book, follow the simple directions for assembling the unit of your choice, and then get back to your hobby.

HIDEAWAY SEWING UNIT

As versatile as the family room itself, this contemporary cabinet works several ways. It's a well-equipped sewing area, a craft and hobby center, a game table for the kids, and a planning desk. For added utility, the unit folds and slides together.

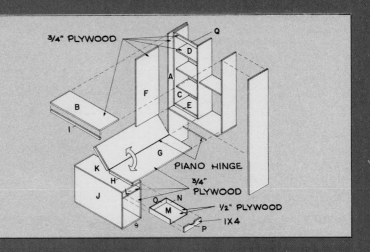

1 Butt-join (page 75) sides (A) and top and counter (B). Fasten to wall with metal angles.

2 Drill holes in sides and divider (C) to receive supports. Butt-join bottom (D), sides (C), facing (E), and top (Q).

3 Hinge door (F) to side of cabinet box (see page 82). Slide unit in space between top and counter (B). Attach facer (I).

4 Slide in the shelves (D).

5 Butt-join sides (J), and top and bottom (K). Position drawer support (L) so top is 3½ inches from top of sides (J). Rout drawer lines on one side (J), if desired. Nail in place.

6 Rabbet (page 76) drawer sides (N) and back (O) ¼ inch to accept bottom. Assemble drawers (M,N, O,P). Cut hand pull.

7 Mount box unit on casters.

8 Hinge tabletop sections (G) together and hinge the right half of table to shelf (B). Add spacers (H).

9 Attach bolt to inside of tabletop. Attach door pulls.

Materials (82x42-in cabinet):

¾-in. plywood—3½ shts.

A	2	16x82 in.
B	2	16x40½ in.
C	3	12x51¼ in.
D	5	11¼x19⅛ in.
E	1	1½x19⅛ in.
F	1	19x48¼ in.
G	2	19⅛x49¾ in.
H	2	1½x19⅛ in.
I	1	1½x40½ in.
J	2	23¾x39 in.
K	2	16x39 in.
L	1	14½x39 in.
Q	1	1½x19⅛ in.

½-in. plywood—½ sht.

M	2	14x18¾ in.
N	4	3½x19 in.
O	2	3½x13½ in.

1x4 pine or fir—4 ft.

P	2	14½ in.

Metal angles, piano and door hinges, adjustable pin-type shelf supports, door pulls, plate swivel casters, surface bolt, glue, and varnish.

INDOOR GARDEN CENTER

If indoor gardening's your game, this unit will get you growing. Slide-out drawers hold potted plants, while the swing-up surface provides a handy work area.

1 Butt-join (see page 75) two sides (C) to bottom (B) using glue and nails. Repeat 4 times.

2 Attach uprights (A) to boxes.

3 Nail left shelf and bottom of storage area (D) in place.

4 Nail ledgers (N) to verticals, and top (D) to ledgers.

5 Attach back (M). Nail support (J) through shelf and back.

6 Attach swing-out support (L) with butt hinges (see page 82).

7 Cover shelf (K) with plastic laminate. Hinge shelf.

8 Butt-join materials (F,G,H,I) to form two boxes.

9 Add door track to storage unit. Paint doors (E); install.

10 Finish, using clear sealer.

Materials (54¼ x 54¼ x 7½-in. unit):

¾-in. plywood—½ sht.
    B 4 6x26 in.   I 2 6x24½ in.
    K 1 14x26 in. J 1 9¼x6¾ in.

½-in. plywood—½ sht.
    M 1 10x54¼ in.

¼-in. hardboard—½ sht.
    E 2 8¼x13¼ in.

1x8 pine or fir—24 ft.
    A 3 54¼ in.   L 1 9¼ in.
    D 3 26 in.

1x4 pine or fir—32 ft.
    C 8 26 in.   G 4 6¾ in.
    F 2 26 in.   H 2 24½ in.

1x2 pine or fir—2 ft.
    N 2 6 in.

Piano and butt hinges, nails, glue, plastic laminate and adhesive, door track, and sealer.

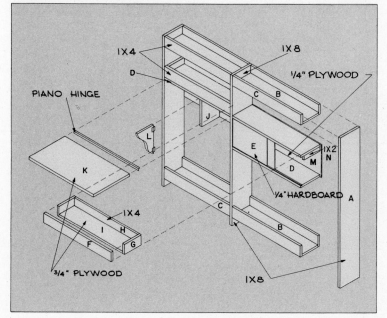

SIMPLE SWING-DOWN SEWING TABLE

This sewing table helps any seamstress stay neat as a pin. It offers ample storage for most projects. Yet, when you'd rather not have your craft in view, the tabletop folds up.

1 Cut a ¼-inch rabbet ⅝ inch deep on back inside edge of pieces A,B,D. Assemble using butt joints.
2 Nail perforated hardboard (C) to back of assembled unit.
3 Nail pieces G,H to bottom of tabletop (E). Apply plastic laminate to top and edges of E.
4 Screw 1x2 ledger (I) to wall studs so top is 28½ inches high.
5 Rest unit (A,B,D) on ledger; fasten to wall using ⅜-inch spacers between hardboard and wall.
6 Attach tabletop to D using a piano hinge.
7 Assemble legs (F,G). Use metal angles to secure mitered corners.
8 Hinge leg unit to tabletop.
9 Install catches, then fill nail holes, and paint.

Materials (30x48-in. table):

¾-in. plywood—½ sht.
  E 1 28¼x45¾ in.
1x6 pine or fir—12 ft.
  A 2 48 in.   B 1 28½ in.
1x4 pine or fir—14 ft.
  F 2 30 in.   H 2 16½ in.
  G 2 28½ in. D 1 28½ in.
1x2 pine or fir—4 ft.
  I 1 28½ in. J 2 2 in.
¼-in. perf. hardboard—½ sht.
  C 1 29¼x47¼ in.
Piano hinges, plastic laminate and adhesive, wood filler, nails, toggle bolts and spacers, magnetic catches, metal angles, glue, and paint.

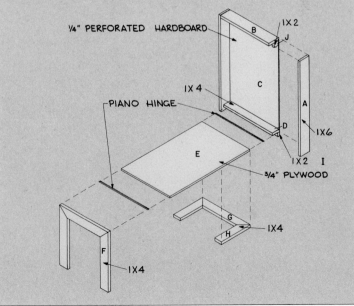

QUICK-AND-EASY PLANT CENTER

This easy-to-make plant center is large enough to give your plants their place in the sun, and at the same time, gives your plant care equipment a place in the shade. It only takes a little space and a sunny window to have green things (even edible ones) growing in your family room all year-round.

1 Build lower storage boxes of 1x12 material. Butt-join (see page 75) the sides (F) and the shelves (G) and secure them with glue and nails. Position the boxes and nail hollow-core door (A) to top of boxes through solid ends of the door.

2 Nail the top (C) between the uprights (B). Nail the center divider (D) to the top. Use a metal angle on either side of the center divider, screwed to the solid part of the door, to hold the center divider plumb.

3 Glue and nail the upper unit shelves (E) in place through the end panels and through the center divider.

4 Complete your project by finishing it with two coats of clear varnish.

Materials (for a 90x81½x30-in. plant center):

1x12 pine or fir—122 ft.

B	2	90 in.
C	1	80 in.
D	1	59¼ in.
E	5	39⅝ in.
F	16	28¼ in.
G	12	23 in.

One 30x80x1¾-in. hollow-core door **(A)**, metal angles, glue, nails, and clear varnish.

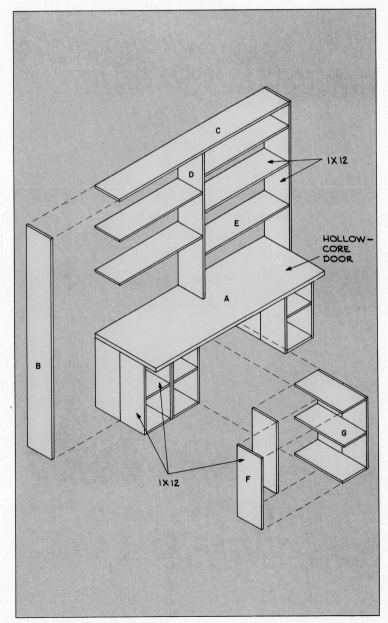

TWO-SIDED CRAFTS CENTER

If storage and work space are what you've always wanted, take heart. This unit gives you both. Each end of the tabletop flips up to reveal storage below, and the lower twin cabinets have ample shelf space concealed behind sliding doors. You'll find the spacious top perfect for laying out fabric, patterns, and other sewing accouterments.

1 Miter corners (see page 77) of base units (A, B) and assemble with glue and nails.

2 Miter all edges of sides (C,E) and top and bottom (D) of storage boxes except those around the door opening. Glue and nail boxes together.

3 Position shelf (F) in center of box. Glue and nail in place from outside.

4 Mount door track at top and bottom of opening. Install finger pulls in doors (G) or drill ¾-inch holes in doors. Slip doors into position.

5 Mount boxes to bases (A,B) using glue and finishing nails. Nail base of top (J) to top of storage boxes (D).

6 Cut ⅜-inch dadoes ¾ inch up from the bottom edge of sides (H,I) to receive top base (J). Use jigsaw to cut hand holes. Miter corners and glue and nail to top.

7 Glue and nail center top piece (K) to side panels (H). Hinge (see page 82) swing-up pieces (L) to center section. The three pieces when hinged together should be flush with the edges of sides.

8 Fill the nail holes and exposed plywood edges. The top of the table may be covered with plastic laminate, if desired. Secure the laminate with adhesive. Then sand unit smooth and paint as desired.

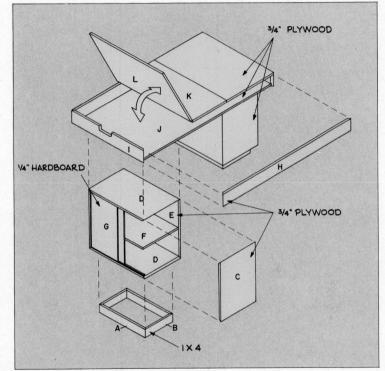

Materials (for a 36x66x34¾-in. crafts table):

¾-in. plywood—3½ shts.
- C 4 18x24½ in.
- D 4 18x28 in.
- E 2 24½x28 in.
- F 2 16x26½ in.
- H 2 6x66 in.
- I 2 6x36 in.
- J 1 35¼x65¼ in.
- K 1 18x36 in.
- L 2 24x36 in.

1x4 pine or fir—14 ft.
- A 4 22½ in. B 4 12½ in.

¼-in. hardboard—½ sht.
- G 4 13½x22½ in.

Pivot hinges, door track, plastic laminate and contact cement, wood filler, glue, nails, and paint.

DESK/ ROOM DIVIDER

There's a heap of storage space in this good-looking desk and room divider. And although it takes a little extra time and careful workmanship to build, this professional-looking piece pays off handsomely with dual-duty service.

1 Insert threaded adjustable legs into metal tubes (A). Construct the frame (A,B,C) as shown in detail 1. Stand frame in place and adjust levelers.

2 Position the top and bottom (E) on metal angles screwed to B,C (see detail 2).

3 Screw long metal angles (D) to uprights (A) as shown, then secure sides (G) to angles by screwing through angles.

4 Rabbet (see page 76) sides (O) and backs (Q) of drawers to receive bottoms (P). Attach fronts (N) and guides.

5 Nail horizontals (F) and back (K) in place. Assemble storage frame (L,R). Attach support for dividers (T) and dividers (U,V,W) using butt joints (page 75). Attach facer (S). Position unit. Attach to back (K).

6 Mount guides on sides (G). Mount doors (I,J) using pivot hinges (page 82). Attach catches.

7 Hinge desk panel (M) to shelf (F). Cover surface with plastic laminate; attach support.

8 Veneer-tape all exposed plywood edges. Stain and varnish.

Materials (for project shown):

¾-in plywood—4 shts.
E	2 19¾x31¾ in.	F	2 20x32 in.
G	2 19¾x77¾ in.	I	2 16x60 in.
H	1 17¾x31¾ in.	J	2 16x36 in.
K	1 23¼x32 in.		
L	1 10x32 in.		
M	1 14¾x32 in.		
N	3 6x32 in.		
O	6 6x20 in.	Q	3 6x29½ in.
R	2 6x14 in.	S	1 2x32 in.

¼-in. plywood—1 sht.
P	3 19⅝x30¼ in.	T	1 6x30½ in.

U	2 6x8 in.	V	5 6x10½ in.
W	2 6x10 in.		

1x1 metal tubing—60 ft.
A	4 107 in.
B	4 32 in.
C	4 20 in.

⅝x⅝ metal angle.
D	4 78 in.

Sheet metal screws, butt and pivot hinges, leaf support, drawer guides, touch latch catches, plastic laminate and adhesive, nails, stain, varnish.

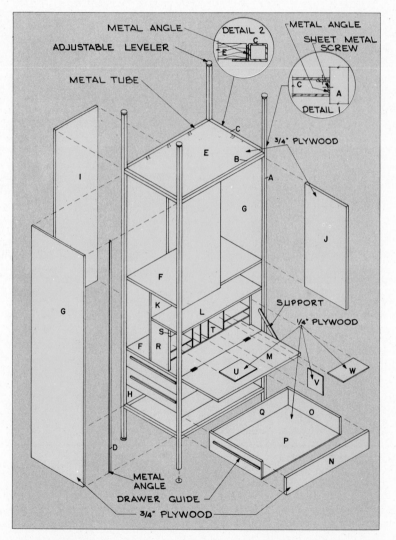

METAL ANGLE

ADJUSTABLE LEVELER

METAL TUBE

DETAIL 2

METAL ANGLE

SHEET METAL SCREW

DETAIL 1

¾" PLYWOOD

METAL ANGLE

DRAWER GUIDE

¾" PLYWOOD

SUPPORT

¼" PLYWOOD

FUN-TO-MAKE CHILDREN'S THINGS

The family room is an ideal place for kids to romp—where they're under a watchful eye and not relegated to solitary confinement in their bedrooms. And, during inclement weather, they can take over the area for an afternoon of play with their friends without destroying the tranquillity of the entire house.

Finding a special place for kids' belongings can be fun, especially when you can build a project to hold all their gear *and* give them organized working and playing space.

Some of these projects are especially adaptable to the changing needs of children. The older set will be interested in projects for hobbies that require a desk or working surface. Other designs, like Charlie's Bank and Sarah's Store, will unleash little imaginations.

In any case, choose washable and durable finishes for your projects, for these buildables will get plenty of hard wear and play.

Give your kids a special area in your family room to call their own. It will make your home a place they'll want to be.

KIDS' WORK AREA

Plan this desk to fit your space, and turn an area of your family room into a study/hobby center for kids only.

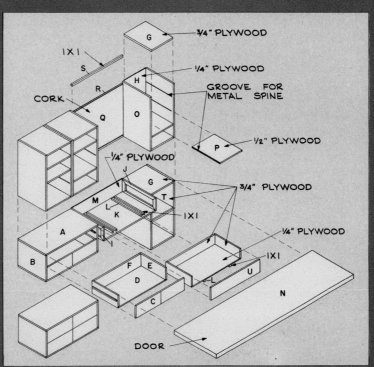

1 Butt-join (see page 75) sides (T) and bottoms and tops (G).

2 Assemble sides (B) and bottoms and tops (A). Add drawer guides.

3 Nail the two hidden backs to right base unit. Nail backs (H) to lower left units.

4 Butt-join sides, bottoms, and tops (G,O) for upper units.

5 Mount spine on box sides and slide shelves (P) in place.

6 Miter and assemble sides (I,J). Attach bottom (K) and back (M). Add drawer guides (L) to K.

7 Screw boxes together. Position center unit; screw together.

8 Rabbet (see page 76) drawer sides and backs (E,F) for bottom (D). Assemble drawers. Attach guides (L) as shown.

9 Cover door (N) with laminate.

10 Glue cork (Q) to back (R); nail to wall. Attach trim (S).

Materials (61¾x80x24-in.):

¾-in. plywood—3½ shts.

A	4	16x30 in.			
B	4	11½x16 in.			
C	5	5⅜x28¼ in.			
E	10	5⅜x15 in.			
F	5	5⅜x25¾ in.			
G	10	13½x16 in.			
I	4	2x8¼ in.	J	4	2x20 in.
K	1	20x28½ in.			
O	6	16x30 in.	T	4	13x16 in.
U	1	7½x28½ in.			

¼-in. plywood—2 shts.

D	5	14⅝x26½ in.
H	5	15x30 in.
	2	15x15 (hidden)
R	1	29¼x30 in.
M	1	8¼x29½ in.

½-in. plywood—½ sht.

P	6	13½x16 in.

1x1 pine or fir—14 ft.

L	6	19 in.	S	2	30 in.

¼-in. cork board

Q	1	28½x30 in.

One 24x80x1¾-in. hollow-core door (N), metal spines, plastic laminate and adhesive, drawer guides, glue, and paint.

DESK
IN A
NICHE

Fit this free-flowing desk in a closet to make a hobby/study center for your kids. Note the height of the lowest shelf—it's just right for seating a child. And don't worry about spills—the laminated shelves are easy to clean.

1 Use a saber saw to cut tops and bottoms (A) for each shelf.
2 Glue blocking (B,C,D,E) to bottoms. Attach ledgers (B,F) to walls, then slip bottoms into position. Nail to ledgers. Glue tops to blocking.
3 Cover tops, bottoms, and facings with plastic laminate.
4 Glue blocking (I,J,L) to desk bottom (G). Notch and rout blocking (K) to receive drawer guides (R). Glue to bottom and screw from below. Attach ledgers (H,M) to walls, then slip bottom in place. Nail to ledgers.

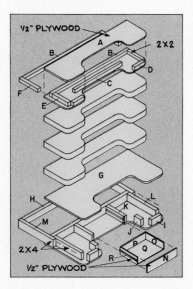

5 Rabbet sides (O) and back (P), and butt-join with front (N). Nail in bottom (Q) and nail guides (R) to drawer sides.
6 Cover top, bottom, and face of unit with plastic laminate.

Materials (24x48x72-in unit):

½-in. plywood—2 shts.
  A 8 14x48 in.   P 1 3½x15 in.
  G 2 24x48 in.
  N 1 4x17 in.
  O 2 3½x10½ in.
2x2 pine or fir—58 ft.

  B 8 45 in.
  C 4 27 in.
  D 8 6 in.   F 8 11 in.
  E 8 9½ in.
2x4 pine or fir—20 ft.
  H 2 45 in.   K 2 11 in.
  I 2 6 in.   L 2 18 in.
  J 2 4 in.   M 2 21 in.
⅛-in. hardboard—½ sht.
  Q 1 10¼x15½ in.
½x½ pine or fir—2 ft.
  R 2 10½ in.

Glue, plastic laminate and adhesive, and nails.

ON-THE-WALL COLLECTION BOXES

Every collection needs room to show off. And your kids' toy, shell, rock, or model plane col- lections will get all the expo- sure they deserve in these sim- ple-to-build boxes.

1 Dado (see page 76) sides (B,H,M) and tops and bottoms (A,G,L) to receive the hardboard backs (D,I,N). Also dado sides (H) to receive ¼-inch hardboard shelves. Miter all joints and glue and nail together. NOTE: bottom of the left cabinet is butt-joined.
2 Nail shelves (C,P) through case sides. Slide shelves (K) in place. Mount metal spine on box sides (B); slide the acrylic shelf (Q) in place.
3 Mount the cases on ledgers (J,O, one hidden under A) to studs. Attach shelves (F).
4 Mount the drop-down door (E) using piano hinge, chains, and magnetic catch.

Materials (48x26x11½-in., 75x 18x11½-in., and 62x32x11½-in. boxes):

1x12 pine or fir—70 ft.
  A 1 26 in.   H 2 75 in.
  B 2 48 in.   L 2 32 in.
  C 2 24½ in. (milled to 9¾ in.)
  F 6 12 in.   G 2 18 in.
  P 4 30½ in. (milled to 10½ in.)
  M 2 62 in.
1x2 pine or fir—6 ft.
  J 1 16½ in.   O 1 30½ in.
    1 24½ in. (hidden under A)
¾-in. plywood—½ sht.
  E 1 21x24½ in.
¼-in. hardboard—1½ shts.
  D 1 25¼x47¼ in.
  I 1 17¼x74¼ in.
  K 7 10½x17¼ in.
  N 1 31¼x61¼ in.
¼-in. acrylic sheet
  Q 1 24½x9¾ in.
Piano hinge, chain, nails, screws, screw eyes, metal spines, magnetic catch, glue, paint.

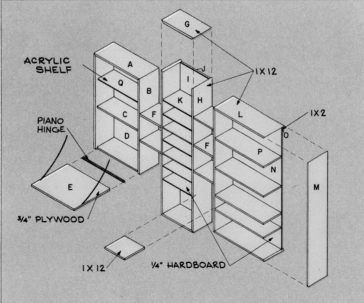

ACRYLIC SHELF

PIANO HINGE

¾" PLYWOOD

1 X 12

¼" HARDBOARD

1 X 12

1 X 2

OFF-THE-FLOOR PLAY SPACE

This play-and-store platform is a great way to keep kids' toys picked up and off the floor. After playtime, the toys are stashed in the three large, floor-level drawers.

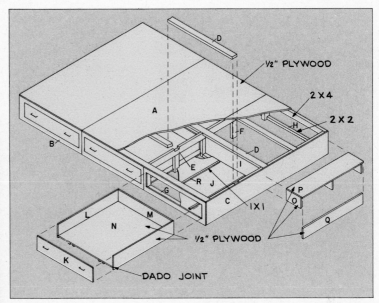

1 To build framework, notch upper 2x4s (E) to receive joists (D). Nail posts (F) to sills (H), sills (G), and notched 2x4s (E). Insert joists (D) and nail.

2 Notch bottoms of drawer units (J) to receive 2x4 posts (F). Nail to 2x2 sills (H) in rear and sill (G) in front. Nail backers (I) to posts and sills.

3 Glue and nail drawer guides (R) to plywood bottoms (J).

4 Dado (see page 76) drawer sides and backs (L,M) to receive plywood bottoms (N). Glue and screw together. Attach drawer fronts (K).

5 Glue and nail plywood fronts (K) and sides (B,C) to framing.

6 Glue and nail top (A) to frame.

7 Nail the tread (P) and the facing (Q) to the step supports (O). Set in place.

Materials (8x12-ft. platform):

½-in. plywood—7 shts.

A	3	4x8 ft.	**B** 3 15½x48 in.
C	3	15½x95½ in.	
I	3	14x45¾ in.	
J	3	47½x47¾ in.	
K	3	11½x45 in.	
P	1	12x48 in.	
L	6	11½x47½ in.	
M	3	11½x44 in.	
N	3	44½x47¼ in.	
O	3	7½x11½ in.	
Q	1	7½x48 in.	

2x4 pine or fir—124 ft.

D	5	11 ft. 11 in.
G	3	45¾ in.
E	4	95½ in.
F	20	12 in.

2x2 pine or fir—48 ft.

H	6	45¾ in.

1x1 pine or fir—72 ft.

R	18	40 in.

Glue, drawer pulls, and paint.

RAINY-DAY
PLAY
STRUCTURES

Nothing's niftier for kids than the world of make-believe. Here, they can spend many an afternoon of fun behind these store fronts. Build them of plywood, or, if desired, use heavy cardboard.

1 Use a saber saw and chisel to make slip joints in panels (A,B,C,D,E). Joints should be equal in length and exactly the thickness of the plywood to ensure a proper fit.

2 For bank, drill nine ½-inch-diameter holes through top panel (C) and lower horizontal (E).

NOTE: For store, eliminate steps 2, 3, and 4.

3 Drill a ½-inch-diameter hole in each block base (G).

4 Slip dowels for teller's cage through holes in panels. Glue a block (G) to each dowel end and tack with wire nail through blocks to dowels.

5 Assemble the structure by slipping the sides (A) and the fronts (B,D) together. Add horizontals (C,E). Paint the unit. For lettering, use a stencil or cut letters from self-adhesive vinyl.

Materials (for a 69x42x24-in. bank or store):

½-in. plywood—1½ shts.
    A 2 24x69 in.
    B 1 25½x36 in.
    C 2 10x42 in.
    D 1 22½x36 in.
    E 1 3x36 in. (bank only)
    G 18 1½x1½ in. (bank only)
½-in.-diameter dowels—14 ft.
    F 9 16 in. (bank only)
Glue and paint.

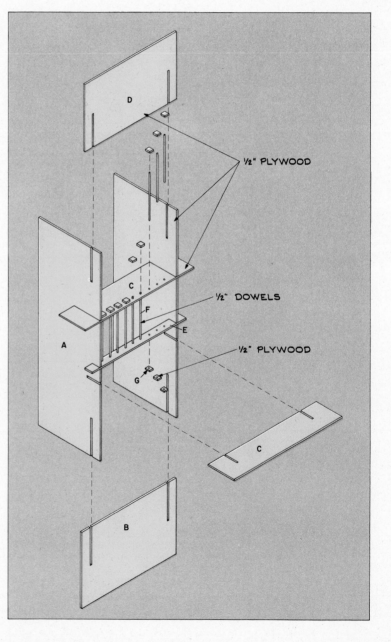

½" PLYWOOD

½" DOWELS

½" PLYWOOD

AROUND-A-WINDOW STUDY CENTER

Give a blank wall a new dimension with this versatile study center. Enclose a window, or brighten up a bare wall with shelves surrounding a center-mounted bulletin board.

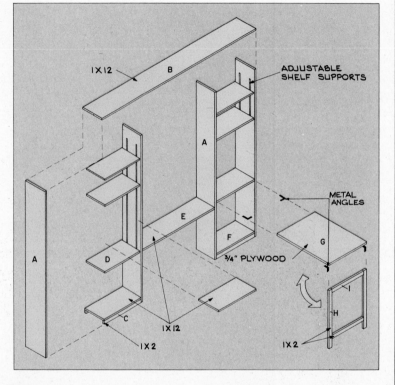

1 Butt-join plates (C) to uprights (A) as shown in sketch.
2 Butt-join top (B) to uprights.
3 Nail the lower shelves (F) to the base plates.
4 Glue and nail shelf E and remaining shelf F in position.
5 Fasten adjustable shelf supports to the verticals. Insert the remaining shelves (D).
6 Surface the entire desk (G) with plastic laminate.
7 Assemble the legs (H,I). Attach one end of the desk to sides (A), the other end to legs, using metal angles.
8 Paint as desired.

9 Attach the unit to the wall with metal angles.

Materials (82x89x11½-in. unit):

¾-in. plywood—½ sht.
  G 1 22½x30 in.

1x12 pine or fir—62 ft.
  A 4 81¼ in.   E 1 41 in.
  B 1 89 in.
  D 6 22 in.
  F 3 22½ in.

1x2 pine or fir—18 ft.
  C 4 22½ in.   I 2 19½ in.
  H 2 28¼ in.

Metal angles, adjustable shelf supports, glue, magnetic catch, plastic laminate and adhesive, and paint.

UNIQUE ENTERTAINING CENTERS

When you're entertaining, guests tend to seek out the most comfortable room in the house. And more often than not, the family room is where you'll find them. It really doesn't matter how formal or casual the occasion may be, the cozy lived-in air of the room puts everyone instantly at ease.

Since the family room is where the action will be, it's smart to have the room subtly decked out with entertaining aids. This chapter is chock-full of projects to lend a helping hand (and some space) to the entertaining essentials—stereo equipment, bar supplies, or serving surfaces.

While not in use, many of these projects fold up to take little space away from the family's everyday action. With organized physical surroundings, entertaining can be hassle-free fun.

If a brush-up on building basics is what you need before tackling these easy-does-it projects, check the back section of the book. You'll be well on your way to entertaining with élan.

STORAGE AND DIVIDER UNIT

This versatile and hard-working unit makes a smashing focal point for any family room. It not only divides the area handsomely, but it also provides open and closed storage to keep the room neat when company calls.

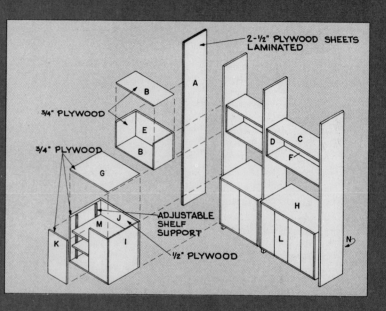

2-½" PLYWOOD SHEETS LAMINATED

¾" PLYWOOD

¾" PLYWOOD

ADJUSTABLE SHELF SUPPORT

½" PLYWOOD

1 Cut plywood to height for verticals (A). Laminate two pieces for each vertical using glue and clamps to hold till dry. Cover all sides with plastic laminate.

2 Miter (see page 77) bottoms, tops, and sides (B,C,D) of upper storage boxes. Assemble using glue and nails. Glue and nail backs (E,F) to boxes.

3 Miter tops, bottoms, and sides (G,H,I) of lower storage units and assemble using glue and nails. Attach backs (J,N).

4 Install clip-type adjustable shelf supports. Insert the shelves (M) on shelf clips.

5 Hinge doors (L,K) (see page 82) to sides of boxes.

6 Paint boxes as desired.

7 Attach one of the verticals (A) to the wall and position an upper and lower storage unit and another vertical next to it. Fasten together with screws. Continue with remaining units.

Materials (for a 96 in. x 8 ft. 10 in. divider):

¾-in. plywood—5 shts.

B	4	16x30 in.
C	2	16x42 in.
D	6	16½x16 in.
G	4	24x30 in.
H	2	24x42 in.
I	6	24x30 in.
K	4	14¼x28½ in.
L	4	10⅛x28½ in.
M	4	22¾x27¾ in.

½-in. plywood—5 shts.

A	8	18x96 in.
E	2	16½x30 in.
F	1	16½x42 in.
J	2	30x30 in.
N	1	30x42 in.

Adjustable shelf supports, hinges, door pulls, plastic laminate and adhesive, paint.

WALL-MOUNTED BAR

Put this easy, inexpensive unit wherever you need the convenience of a wall-hung cabinet. Better yet, build two: use one for a bar, and one as a desk by the telephone.

1 Rabbet (see page 76) back edges of sides (A,B). Miter (see page 77) all corners and assemble using glue and nails.
2 Glue and nail back (E) in rabbet joint.
3 Insert the shelf (C); nail through sides of the box.
4 Miter the corners of the L channel metal trim. Run a glue bead in channel and slip door (D) into channel. Clamp and allow to dry thoroughly. Mark channel for screws of piano hinge and drill pilot holes. Apply hinge to the shelf and to door (see page 82).
5 Cut chain to length so door is level when open. Use screw eyes to hold chain to door and inside of box. Attach a magnetic catch if the door does not fit snugly.
6 Sand unit smooth. Countersink nails and fill all nail holes with wood putty. Paint unit.

Materials (20x20x9½-in. bar):
1x10 pine or fir—10 ft.
    A 2 20 in.
    B 2 20 in.
    C 1 18½ in.
       (milled to 8½ in. wide)
¾-in. plywood—½ sht.
    D 1 13¼x18¼ in.
¼-in. plywood—½ sht.
    E 1 19¼x19¼ in.
Piano hinge, L channel metal trim, chain, screw eyes, glue, nails, paint, magnetic catch (optional).

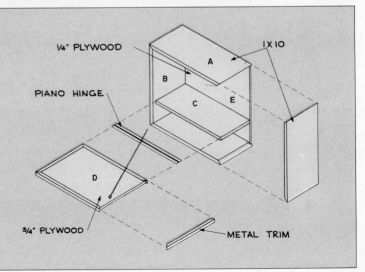

MULTI-MEDIA DIVIDER

Use this entertainment center to house all of your electronic equipment. The freestanding divider is simple to build and acts as a buffer between TV viewers and active play areas.

1 Cut dadoes in sides (B) to receive shelf supports. Miter top and sides (A,B). Nail top (A) to ceiling joists.

2 Stand sides (B) upright and nail to top (A).

3 Insert back (C) and lower shelf (D); nail in place. Fasten shelf support in dado and slide in the other two shelves.

4 Cut quarter round (E,F) for trim at ceiling. Miter and nail in place.

5 Paint unit and shelves.

Materials (for a 96x48x30-in. divider):

¾-in. plywood—4½ shts.
- A 1 30x48 in.
- B 2 30x96 in.
- C 1 46½x95¼ in.
- D 3 46½x29¼ in.

½-in. face quarter round—16 ft.
- E 2 49 in. F 2 31 in.

Adjustable shelf supports and clips, glue, and paint.

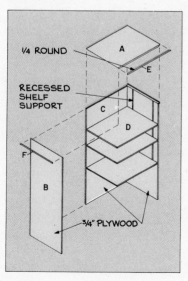

MODULAR STORAGE BANQUETTES

For the ultimate in storage systems, this unit has it all. Each section is a freestanding unit of open and closed storage. If you have stereo speakers to conceal, face two sections with plywood and make cutouts backed with fabric, as was done here.

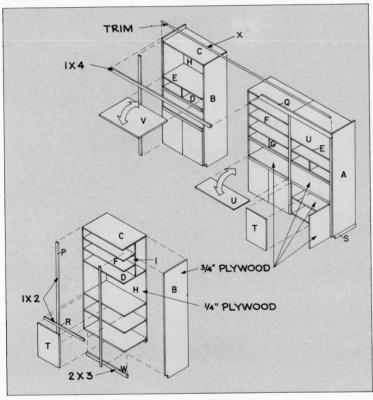

1 Build one unit at a time. Start with the left unit shown pulled out in the drawing. Glue and screw together the vertical sides, top, and bottom (B,C,D) using butt joints (see page 75). Note that B is notched to allow for toe space.

2 Attach base (W) at front and back of verticals. Glue and screw top shelf (D) in place.

3 Glue and nail back (H) to sides, bottom, and shelf.

4 Position the divider (I) between the shelf (D) and the top. Fasten securely in place.

5 Glue and screw remaining shelves (F,D) in place.

6 Glue and nail trim (P,R) to side panels and first shelf of lower section.

7 Hinge (see page 82) the doors (T) to the verticals. Attach the door pulls.

8 Build other units using same techniques as in steps 1 through 7. For fold-down doors (U,V), use three butt hinges and magnetic catches. Screw all units together, and apply chrome strips and head and base trim.

9 Paint units as desired.

Materials (for a 96 in. x 14 ft. 10-in. storage wall):

¾-in. plywood—15 shts.

A	2	18x96 in.
B	8	18x92½ in.
C	4	18x44 in.

D	16	17¾x42½ in.		H	4	42½x92½ in.		W	8	42½ in.
E	2	18½x42½ in.		I	1	29¼x42½ in.		1-in. chrome strip—40 ft.		
F	6	12x42½ in.		1x2 pine or fir—68 ft.				Trim—to match existing		
G	3	9¼x12 in.		P	5	92½ in.		S	2	18 in.
T	8	21¼x30 in.		R	7	42½ in.		X	1	14 ft. 10 in.
U	4	19¼x42½ in.		1x4 pine or fir—16 ft.						
V	1	30x42½ in.		Q	1	14 ft. 9½ in.				
¼-in. plywood—4 shts.				2x3 pine or fir—32 ft.						

Butt hinges, glue, screws, nails, door pulls, and paint.

EASY-UPKEEP PENINSULA BAR

This bar, complete with "brass rail," turns a corner of the room into a family refreshment stand. Your youngsters will have great fun using it for a soda fountain, and you'll find it especially handy for mixing drinks for the gang.

1 Assemble base (D,E) with butt joints (see page 75) using glue and screws. Glue and screw bottom (C) to base.
2 For storage units, dado (see page 76) sides (F) for shelves. Run glue bead in dadoes and screw shelves (I,J) into side panel dadoes.
3 Position units on base (C). Toenail storage units to hold in place. Attach back (B).
4 Nail end panel (A) to bottom (C) and back (B). Apply ledger (G) even with dado in opposite panel (F). Attach shelf (H). Apply facing ledger (N) at upper edge of panel (A).
5 Glue and nail counter surface (K) and trim (L) together. The trim edge should be flush with top of the plywood. Lay the counter over the base units; glue and nail into position.
6 Assemble bar counter (O) and trim (L) with glue and nails. Apply bar ledger (M) to wall with glue and nails; nail bar counter to ledger (M), back (B), and end panel (A).
7 Hinge doors (P,Q) (see page 82) to edge of sides using two butt hinges on each door. Drill doors for pulls. Install pulls and magnetic door catches.
8 Cover the counters and trim (K,O,L,N) with plastic laminate.

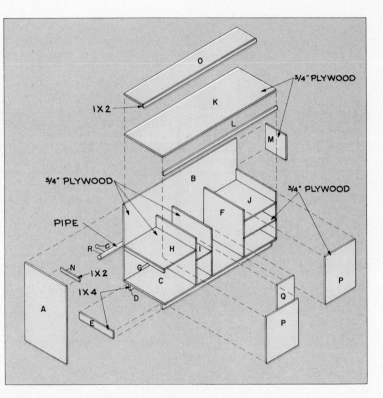

Paint cabinets, doors, and cabinet interior. Mount the foot rail (R) to the front of the unit.

Materials (for a 42x66x24-in. bar):

¾-in. plywood—3½ shts.

A	1	24x38½ in.
B	1	38½x65¼ in.
C	1	22½x65¼ in.
F	4	22½x25 in.
H	1	18¼x22½ in.
I	1	9½x22½ in.
J	2	17¾x22½ in.
K	1	22½x65¼ in.
M	1	10½x11¼ in.
O	1	10½x65¼ in.
P	2	18x25 in.
Q	1	9¾x25 in.

1x2 pine or fir—16 ft.

G	1	22½ in.
L	2	65¼ in.
N	1	12 in.

1x4 pine or fir—16 ft.

D	2	60¾ in.
E	2	19 in.

2- or 2½-in. chromed pipe

R	1	65 in.

Pivot hinges, plastic laminate and adhesive, paint, glue, screws, nails, magnetic catches, door pulls, and supports and endcaps for chromed pipe.

This fold-out buffet table holds everything from hors d'oeuvres to holiday fare with equal ease. The top is hinged to fold to half its size, and the entire unit rests on swivel casters for easy movement to and from any location.

1 To assemble base, butt-join (see page 75) bottom (D) and facing (B) using glue and screws. Cover bottom (D) with plastic laminate. Glue and nail caster blocks (C) near corners of bottom. Drill blocks for ball-type stem casters. Attach casters.

2 Glue and nail 1x1 drawer guides to drawer base (F) and 1x1 and 1x2 sliding top guides (L,M) to facings (B).

3 Hinge (see page 82) the sliding top (P) with piano hinge. Then cover top and the edges with plastic laminate.

4 Glue and nail the 1x1s and the 1x2s for insertion guides (N,O) to the underside of one top section (P).

5 Assemble drawer base (F) and facings (B) using butt joints. Nail one side panel (A) to base unit (B,D) and to top section (B,F). Prop up loose end.

6 Insert tabletop guides (N,O) into guides on facings (L,M). Close top and glue and screw other end panel (A) in place.

7 Cut hand pull in drawer front (H) with coping saw. Dado (see page 76) sides and back (I,J) 1 inch up from bottom edge to receive drawer bottom (K). Assemble drawer (H,I,J,K) using glue and screws. Glue and nail 1x1 drawer guides (G) to bottom of drawer.

8 Attach adjustable shelf supports to sides of cart. Insert shelf (E).

9 Sand smooth and finish the base of the unit with two coats of polyurethane.

Materials (37½x36x24-in. cart).

¾-in. plywood—2 shts.
A 2 22½x35 in.
B 4 7½x34½ in.
D 1 19½x34½ in.
E 1 19½x34 in.
F 1 18x34½ in.
H 1 5x20 in.   I 2 5x18 in.
J 1 5x18½ in.
P 2 24x37½ in.

¼-in. plywood—½ sht.
K 1 17½x19 in.

2x2 pine or fir—2 ft.
C 4 5 in.

1x2 pine or fir—10 ft.
M 2 34½ in.   O 2 17¼ in.

1x1 pine or fir—20 ft.
G 6 18 in.   N 2 17¼ in.
L 2 34½ in.

Adjustable shelf supports, piano hinge, casters, glue, plastic laminate and adhesive, and polyurethane.

Figure labels: ¾" PLYWOOD, P, N, O, L, 1X1, ADJUSTABLE SHELF SUPPORT, M, 1X1, G, ¾" PLYWOOD, F, B, 1X2, E, J, K, A, 2X2, D, I, B, C, ¼" PLYWOOD, H, G, CASTER, 1X1 DRAWER GUIDE

FOLD-OUT BAR AND SERVER

This handsome freestanding bar doubles its work space in a jiffy. Both sides of the top are hinged to lift up and out, giving you plenty of serving area for any get-together.

1 Glue and screw the ledgers (H) to the sides (A). Top ledger should be ¾ inch below the upper edge of sides; the bottom ledger 15 inches below.

2 Set shelves (B) on ledgers (H); glue and screw in place. Glue and nail facing (C) to shelves.

3 Butt-join (see page 75) sides of fold-out boxes (D,E) using 2x2 blocks for nailers (F). Screw the tops and bottoms (G) into place on the 2x2 blocks.

4 Attach boxes with piano hinges (see page 82) to sides (A).

5 Apply plastic laminate to boxes and to shelves (B). Apply veneer tape to plywood edges.

6 Paint hardboard front and apply polyurethane to plywood.

Materials (for a 36x40x18-in. fold-out bar):

¾-in. plywood—1 sht.
   A 2 18x36 in.
   B 2 16¼x34½ in.
   D 4 4x18 in.
   E 4 4x16½ in.

½-in. plywood—½ sht.
   G 4 16½x16½ in.

¼-in. hardboard—½ sht.
   C 1 16x34½ in.

2x2 pine or fir—2 ft.
   F 8 2¾ in.

1x1 pine or fir—6 ft.
   H 4 16 in.

Piano hinges, plastic laminate, adhesive, glue, veneer tape, paint, and polyurethane.

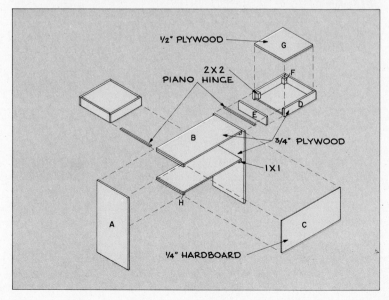

½" PLYWOOD   G
2X2   PIANO HINGE   F
E   D
B   ¾" PLYWOOD
1X1
A   H   C
¼" HARDBOARD

DROP-FRONT BUFFET WITH STORAGE

The good looks of this buffet alone can justify adding it to your family room. But for those **with a practical side, the unit is loaded with hidden storage and it's also simple to make.**

1 Cut top, bottom, sides, and back (A,B,C). Notch top and bottom (B) ¾ inch deep and 77 inches long for door recess. NOTE: Center 77-inch notch length for a 38½-inch notch on each side of center. Assemble the basic box using mitered joints (see page 77).

2 Cut doors (E) and end facing panels (D) from plywood. Hinge doors (E) to bottom shelf (B) using butt hinges (see page 82). Install magnetic catch hardware to the doors and to the buffet top. Nail the end panels (D) into place. Then, countersink and fill all of the nail holes.

3 Cut and miter wrap-around 1x4s (G,H). Cut spacers (F,). Glue and nail spacers (F) to the edge of top and bottom. Cover spacers with trim (G) by gluing and nailing. Attach horizontal trim (H) to plywood top and bottom with glue and nails. Countersink all nail holes and fill with putty to match stain color.

4 Stain the trim and paint plywood as desired.

Materials (for a 15½x96x9½-in. buffet):

¾-in. plywood—1 sht.
A 1 14x96 in.
B 2 8¾x96 in.
C 2 8¾x14 in.
D 2 9½x14 in.
E 4 14x16⅝ in.

1x4 pine or fir—20 ft.
F 3 14 in.
G 5 15½ in.
H 10 9½ in.

Butt hinges, magnetic catches, glue, nails, wood filler, stain, and paint.

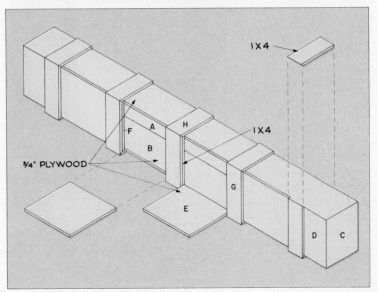

POTPOURRI OF FAMILY ROOM PROJECTS

If your family spends most of its free time in the family room, it just makes sense to surround yourselves with the comfortable things that can make your casual living space more enjoyable. These projects were chosen to do just that, and to help you fill the room with utilitarian yet good-looking furnishings at the same time.

Some of these designs bring new life to your family room houseplants. Whether you have a few special specimens or a roomful of growing things, you'll find a project here to help you showcase them in style. Some add supplemental lighting to green up an empty corner; others transform a window into a special showy area.

If furniture is a problem for you, you'll find a whole roomful of table and seating projects that are a snap to build. Or, if you need just a few occasional pieces, there are several to choose from.

And best of all, every one of these handsome projects is family-proof, designed to withstand the heavy use befitting the major activity space of your home.

LIGHTED INTERIOR GARDEN

Turn a corner of your family room into a veritable jungle with this special plant environment. Your favorite flora will flourish under the fluorescent grow lights.

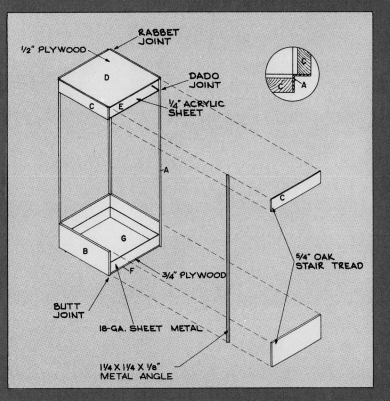

1 Drill metal angles (A) for screws; attach to frame (B). Butt-join (see page 75) bottom (F) and sides (B).

2 Rabbet (see page 76) the top of the sides (C) and dado (see page 76) ¼ inch up from bottom. Screw metal angles to three sides (C).

3 Bend diffuser (E) into dado. Screw fourth side (C) in place.

4 Mount fixtures. Gang wire and drill through angle for cord.

5 Notch corners of D to fit around angles. Rest top (D) in rabbet.

6 Drop metal pan in bottom. Finish oak with polyurethane.

Materials (84x30¼x30¼ in. stand):

5/4 oak stair tread—20 ft.
   B 4 12x27½ in.
   C 4 6x27½ in.

½-in. plywood—½ sht.
   D 1 28x28 in.

¾-in. plywood—½ sht.
   F 1 27½x27½ in.

¼-in. sheet acrylic
   E 1 28x28 in.

1¼x1¼x⅛-in. metal angle
   A 4 84 in.

One 40x40-inch piece 18-gauge sheet metal (G), screws, nails, fluorescent fixtures and cord, and polyurethane.

COMBINATION TABLE AND PLANTER

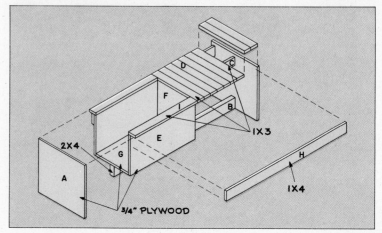

This dual-purpose project lets you show off your special house-plants as well as provide extra seating. Line the planter with fiber glass or sheet metal to waterproof the box.

1 To construct the box, glue and nail sides (E,F) and bottom (G) together using butt joints (see page 75). Nail ends (A) to horizontal base stretcher (B). Prop box (E,F,G) in place; nail to base stretcher (B) and through end panels (A).
2 Nail center brace (C) in place through end panel (A) and box side (F).
3 Nail the edgers (H) along each side of unit level with center brace (C).
4 Glue and nail seat slats (D) to edgers (H) and center brace (C). Countersink nails; fill with wood filler.
5 Paint all plywood and finish redwood with one or more coats of polyurethane. Line the planter box as desired.

Materials (for a 16x48x16-in. table/planter):

¾-in. plywood—½ sht.
  A 2 16x16 in.
  E 2 11¾x24¾ in.
  F 1 11¾x11 in.
  G 1 11x24 in.
2x4 redwood—4 ft.
  B 1 46½ in.
1x4 redwood—8 ft.
  H 2 46½ in.
1x3 redwood—22 ft.
  C 1 21¾ in.
  D 9 16 in.
  I 2 24 in.
Nails, polyurethane, wood filler, and sheet metal or fiber glass.

FLOOR-LEVEL PLANT PLATFORM

This plant patio combines the practicality of an outdoor garden with the pleasantries of an indoor one. The frame is built around half-inch paving bricks, and its exterior dimensions can be adjusted to accommodate bricks of any size.

1 Rabbet (see page 76) frame (B,C) for bottom (A). Miter corners (see page 77) and assemble. Nail bottom (A) in rabbet.
2 Nail cap (D,E), to frame.
3 Lay bricks in a bed of mastic. Sprinkle sand in joints.

Materials (63x27-in. planter):

1x4 redwood—16 ft.
    B 2 61½ in. **C** 2 25½ in.
1x2 redwood—16 ft.
    D 2 63 in. **E** 2 27 in.
½-in. plywood—1 sht.
    A 1 60½x24½ in.
Brick pavers, nails, tile mastic, sand, and polyurethane.

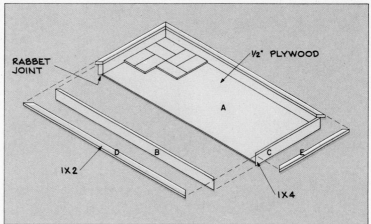

BI-LEVEL POTTED PLANT STAND

Back-lit by a window, this sleek-lined structure lets all the attention focus on the bountiful plant display. Fiber glass coating on the tray eliminates the possibility of water leakage.

1 To construct the base, half-notch the long stretcher (C) and legs (D) for slip joint. Slip together and toenail.

2 Rabbet (see page 76) frame (E,F) to receive bottom (G). Miter (see page 77) corners of frame; glue and nail. Insert bottom (G) in rabbet; nail.

3 Drill ¾-inch holes in horizontal (A) for hangers. Drill holes in channels (B) and screw to horizontal. Screw bottoms of channels to base (C).

4 Nail together framed bottom (E,F,G) and base (C,D).

5 Coat inside of framed bottom with fiber glass or with coats of polyurethane. Add a layer of pea gravel under pots. Finish remainder of unit with a single coat of polyurethane.

Materials (for a 60x18x90-in. plant stand):

¾-in. plywood—1 sht.
   C 1 13½x60 in.
   D 2 13½x18 in.
½-in. plywood—1 sht.
   G 1 17x57½ in.
1x6 redwood—6 ft.
   A 1 60 in.
1x3 redwood—14 ft.
   E 2 58½ in. F 2 18 in.
1x1x1x⅛ aluminum channel
   B 2 90 in.
Fiber glass, polyurethane, nails, screws, and pea gravel.

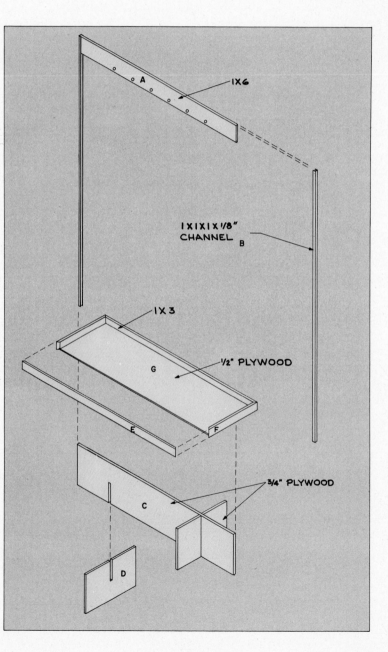

WOOD SCULPTURE TABLE

The good clean looks of glass combined with the stability of an interlocked wood base make this coffee table a smashing addition to any family room. Substitute acrylic sheet for the glass tabletop if you have active youngsters around.

1 Half-notch base supports (H,I) to receive crossmembers (B,C). Glue and nail ledgers (G) to two of the base supports (H) at bottom of notch.

2 Notch, glue, and nail stretcher (E) to ledgers (G).

3 Notch stretcher (C) to receive 2x6s (B). Glue and nail 1x1 (F) between stretcher (C) and stretcher (D).

4 Insert B and C in notches.

6 Paint base; add glass (A).

Materials (36x78x16-in. table):

2x6 pine or fir—6 ft.
   B 2 30 in.
2x8 pine or fir—6 ft.
   E 1 56½ in.   I 1 15 in.
2x12 pine or fir—4 ft.
   H 3 15 in.
1x6 pine or fir—10 ft.
   C 1 58 in.   D 1 56½ in.
1x1 pine or fir—6 ft.
   F 1 53 in.   G 2 9 in.
One 36x78x1-in. piece glass or acrylic sheet (A), glue, and paint.

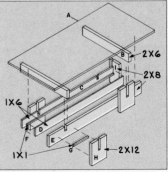

LIGHTED DISPLAY STAND

An illuminated end table makes any group of collectibles "glow from within." Adjust the height and depth of the unit to coordinate with the scale of your furnishings.

1 Butt-join (see page 75) sides (A) and ends (B).
2 Drop bottom (C) into box and nail in place.
3 Glue and nail ledgers (E,F) to sides and ends of box.
4 Install six gang-wired porcelain sockets — three per side — 6 inches down from top.
5 Drill hole for plug wire in end of box. Wire sockets and install 25-watt bulbs.
6 Insert top (D). Paint unit as desired.

Materials (for a 39x18x30-in. stand):

¾-in. plywood—1½ shts.
　A 2 30x39 in.
　B 2 16½x29¼ in.
　C 1 16½x39 in.
1x1 pine or fir—10 ft.
　E 2 37½ in.
　F 2 15 in.
½-in. frosted acrylic sheet
　D 1 16½x37½ in.
Porcelain light sockets, glue, nails, plug wire and fittings, and paint.

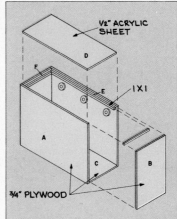

PARQUET-TOPPED TABLE

This streamlined step-top table solves the where-to-put-your-plants problem. Or, without the tier, it doubles as a handsome coffee table. The prefinished wood parquet blocks are easy to work with and are extremely durable.

1 Glue and screw ledgers (C) to rails (B). Attach end panels (A). Nail top (D) to ledgers (C) and ends (A).
2 Glue parquet blocks.
3 Build small stand (E,F,G) in same manner as table.
4 Paint exposed wood.

Materials (48x19½x16-in. table):
¾-in. plywood—1 sht.

A 2 16x19½ in.
D 1 18x46½ in.
E 2 6x7½ in. G 1 6x24 in.
1x1 pine or fir—8 ft.
C 2 46½ in.
1x3 pine or fir—4 ft.
F 2 24 in.
1x4 pine or fir—8 ft.
B 2 46½ in.
Glue, nails, prefinished parquet blocks, and paint.

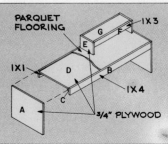

TILE-SURFACED TABLE

Tile-topped tables like this one can withstand the hardest of wear and they're a snap to **make. Build several — you'll wonder how your family room ever managed without them.**

1 Notch base panels (B) for slip joint. Slip base together and nail for stability.
2 Glue and nail nailers (C) to inside of base, flush with top edges. Attach top (A).
3 Use ceramic tile mastic to set tiles. Grout tile.
4 Miter corners (see page 77) of trim (D); glue and nail.
5 Paint table.

Materials (for an 18½x18½x13-in. table):
½-in. plywood—½ sht.
   A 1 18x18 in.
   B 2 12x24 in.
1x1 pine or fir—6 ft.
   C 8 8 in.
¼x¾ screen bead—8 ft.
   D 4 18½ in.
Ceramic tile, mastic, grout, glue, nails, and paint.

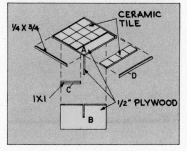

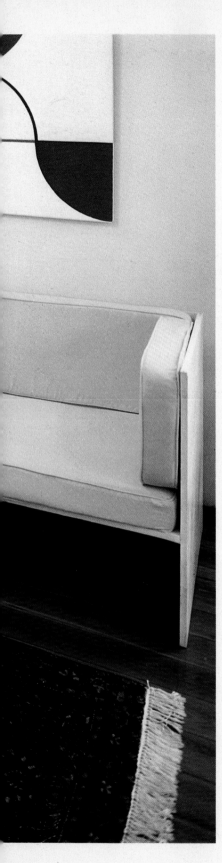

QUICK-AND-EASY SOFA, CHAIR, TABLE

Building this roomful of furniture may look like a big undertaking, but it's really no more than a weekend's work. And the results are surprisingly comfy. Use four-inch-thick foam pads for seat backs and cushions, and cover them with brightly colored fabric.

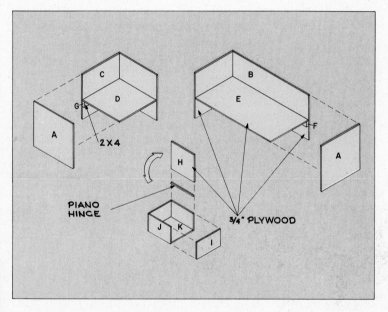

1 To assemble the sofa, glue and screw the ledger (F) to the back panel (B) 14 inches from the floor for comfortable seat height. Use flat head screws and countersink. Fill with wood filler and sand smooth.

2 Glue and screw the side panels (A) to the back (B) using butt joints (see page 75).

3 Insert the seat (E) and screw it to the ledger and through the sides (A).

4 To build the chair, screw ledger (G) to back (C) 14 inches from floor. Glue and screw side panels (A) to back (C). Attach seat (D) as done for sofa.

5 To build the flip-top box table, glue and screw together the sides (I,J) using butt joints. Insert the bottom (K) and nail through sides.

6 Fasten piano hinge to top edge of one side panel and attach top (H) to piano hinge.

7 Paint units as desired and add covered foam cushions.

Materials (for a 60x30x30-in. sofa, a 30x30x30-in. chair, and an 18x18x12-in. table):

¾-in. plywood—3 shts.
- A 4 30x30 in.
- B 1 30x58½ in.
- C 1 30x28½ in.
- D 1 28½x29¼ in.
- E 1 58½x29¼ in.
- H 1 18x18 in.
- I 2 11¼x18 in.
- J 2 11¼x16½ in.
- K 1 16½x16½ in.

2x4 pine or fir—8 ft.
- F 1 58½ in.   G 1 28½ in.

Piano hinge, glue, screws, paint, and covered cushions.

PLANNING AND BUILDING BASICS

Building things the right way isn't any more difficult than muddling your way through a project without direction. That's why it's so important for you to read the information in this final section of the book.

You'll find answers to all of your construction questions. And there's plenty of advice on waterproofing your basement, installing a suspended ceiling or a fireplace, erecting a partition wall, plus much more.

COMMON CONSTRUCTION MATERIALS

The materials you use for construction will vary, depending on the item's intended use. So when making your selection, ask yourself these questions: Are you constructing something for indoor or outdoor use? Is the item strictly utilitarian, or will it be suitable for use in a living room? Is it intended for light-duty use, or will it be a long-lived project subject to considerable use—and abuse?

Hardboard

Hardboard is available in 4x8-foot sheets and comes in ⅛- and ¼-inch thicknesses. Standard hardboard is an excellent choice for cabinetwork, drawer bottoms, and concealed panels.

You can also get hardboard perforated with holes spaced about one inch apart. Perforated hardboard is recommended for building storage for soiled laundry and for the backs of hi-fi cabinets. The quarter- and eighth-inch perforated hardboard lends itself to storing garden equipment and tools, too, as its holes accept hooks designed for this purpose. To expand or change the arrangement, just switch the hooks around. If the project will be subject to dampness, use tempered hardboard.

Particle board, chip board, and flake board, also members of the hardboard family, have a coarser grain structure, are lighter in color, and are available in thicknesses up to ¾ inch. These products are made of granulated or shredded wood particles forced together under pressure with a binder at high temperatures.

Plywood

Plywood also comes in 4x8-foot sheets, though larger sheets are available on special order. Thicknesses range from ⅛-inch to ¾-inch. For light-duty storage, the ¼- and ½-inch thicknesses are adequate. If you are planning to build an outdoor storage unit, specify *exterior grade* when making your purchase. Exterior grade plywood has its layers glued together with a waterproof glue to withstand rain.

The surfaces of plywood sheets are graded A, B, C, and D—with A the smoother, better surface and D the least desirable appearance. Choose AA (top grade, both sides) only for projects where both sides will be exposed; use a less expensive combination for others.

Solid Wood

Plain, ordinary wood still ranks as the most popular building material. Wood is sold by the "board foot" (1x12x12 inches). One board foot equals the surface area of one square foot, with a nominal thickness of one inch.

Wood is marketed by "grade." For most building projects No. 2 grade will satisfy your needs. This grade may have some blemishes, such as loose knots, but these don't reduce the strength of the wood.

If you're planning to build a unit that will be part of a room's decor, you should buy *select lumber*—a grade that's relatively free of blemishes.

Remember, too, that outdoor projects are a different subject.

Redwood or cedar is preferable, but if you use a soft wood such as fir, be sure to treat it for moisture resistance.

You can buy boards up to 16 feet in length and 12 inches in width, though occasionally a lumberyard may have somewhat wider or longer boards.

Wood is divided into two categories. Softwoods, used commonly for general construction, come from trees that don't shed their leaves in the winter: hemlock, fir, pine, spruce, and similar evergreen cone-bearing trees. Hardwoods come from trees that do shed their leaves: maple, oak, birch, mahogany, walnut, and other broad-leaved varieties.

All lumber is sold by a nominal size. A 2x4, for example, does not measure two by four inches. It's actually 1½x3½ inches (though the nominal *length* of a 2x4 is usually its true length). The drawing shows nominal sizes, as well as the actual sizes, of most pieces of common lumber.

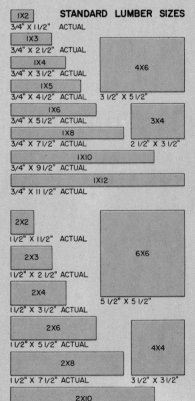

STANDARD LUMBER SIZES

1X2	3/4" X 1 1/2" ACTUAL
1X3	3/4" X 2 1/2" ACTUAL
1X4	3/4" X 3 1/2" ACTUAL
1X5	3/4" X 4 1/2" ACTUAL
1X6	3/4" X 5 1/2" ACTUAL
1X8	3/4" X 7 1/2" ACTUAL
1X10	3/4" X 9 1/2" ACTUAL
1X12	3/4" X 11 1/2" ACTUAL

4X6 — 3 1/2" X 5 1/2"
3X4 — 2 1/2" X 3 1/2"

2X2	1 1/2" X 1 1/2" ACTUAL
2X3	1 1/2" X 2 1/2" ACTUAL
2X4	1 1/2" X 3 1/2" ACTUAL
2X6	1 1/2" X 5 1/2" ACTUAL
2X8	1 1/2" X 7 1/2" ACTUAL
2X10	1 1/2" X 9 1/2" ACTUAL
2X12	1 1/2" X 11 1/2" ACTUAL

6X6 — 5 1/2" X 5 1/2"
4X4 — 3 1/2" X 3 1/2"

WOOD JOINTS YOU SHOULD KNOW

No matter what material you're planning to use, it will have to be cut to size—measure twice and cut once is a good rule—then put together using glue, nails or screws, and one of these joints.

Butt Joints

The simplest joint of all, the butt joint, consists of two pieces of wood meeting at a right angle and

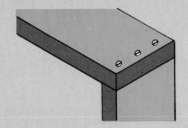

held together with nails, or preferably, screws (see sketch). A dab of glue before using the nails or screws will make the joint even more secure. But don't use glue if you're planning to take the work apart sometime later.

When reinforced by one of the six methods illustrated, the butt joint is effective for making corner

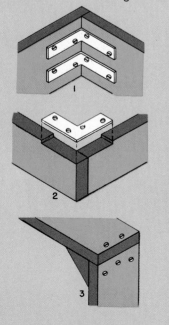

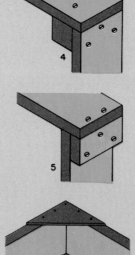

joints. Two common fasteners are angle irons (1), and flat corner plates (2). Using scrap wood, you can reinforce the joint with a triangular wedge (3), or with a square block (4). A variation of the square block places the block on the outside of the joint (5). Finally, a triangular gusset made from plywood or hardboard will also serve to reinforce a corner butt joint (6).

When a butt joint is in the form of a T—for example, in making a framework for light plywood or hardboard—you can reinforce it with an angle iron, T plate, or corrugated fasteners.

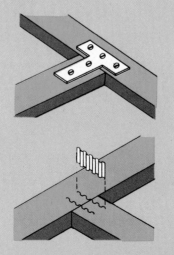

For really rough work, you can drive in a couple of nails at an

angle, or toenail (see sketch). A variation of this is to place a block of wood alongside the crosspiece

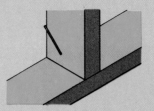

and secure it with a couple of nails.

A close cousin to the T joint and the butt joint is the plain overlap joint. It is held in place with at least two screws (see sketch). For extra reinforcement, apply glue between the pieces of wood.

Butt joints are an excellent means of securing backs to various units, especially when appearance is not a factor. Simply cut the back to the outside di-

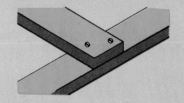

mensions of the work, then nail in place . . . it's called a flush back.

Lap Joints

On those projects where appearance is vital, consider full and half-lap joints. To make a full lap joint, cut a recess in one of the pieces of wood equal in depth to the thickness of the crossmember (see sketch).

The half-lap joint is similar to the full lap joint when finished, but the technique is different. First, cut a recess equal to half the

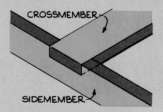

thickness of the crossmember halfway through the crossrail. Then, make a similar cut in the opposite half of the other piece (see sketch on the next page).

Butt joints and overlap joints do

not require any extra work besides cutting the pieces to size. However, full and half-lap joints

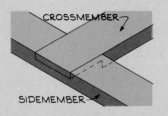

require the use of a backsaw and a chisel. For a full-lap joint, mark off the thickness and width of the crossmember on the work in which it is to fit.

Use the backsaw to make a cut at each end that's equal to the thickness of the crossmember, then use a chisel to remove the wood between the backsaw cuts. Check for sufficient depth and finish off with a fine rasp or sandpaper. Apply white glue to the mating surfaces and insert two screws to hold the joint securely.

Dado Joints

The dado joint is a simple way of suspending a shelf from its side supports. To make a dado joint, draw two parallel lines with a knife

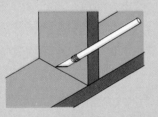

across the face of the work equal to the thickness of the wood it is to engage (see sketch). The depth should be about one-third of the thickness of the wood.

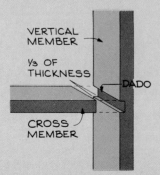

Next, make cuts on these lines and one or more between the lines

with a backsaw. Then, chisel out the wood to the correct depth.

You can speed the job immeasurably by using a router, a bench saw, or a radial arm saw. Any one of these power tools makes the cutting of dadoes an easy job — and provides much greater accuracy than can be achieved by hand.

If appearance is a factor, consider the stopped dado joint. In this type of joint, the dado (the cutaway part) extends only part way, and only a part of the shelf is cut away to match the non-cut part of the dado.

To make a stopped dado, first make your guide marks and chisel away a small area at the stopped end to allow for saw movement. Then make saw cuts

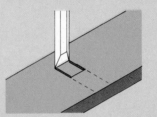

along your guide marks to the proper depth. Next chisel out the waste wood as shown in sketch.

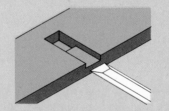

And finally, cut away a corner of the connecting board to accommodate the stopped dado.

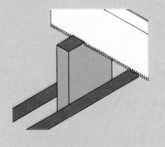

Rabbet Joints

The rabbet joint is really a partial dado. As you can see in the drawing at the top of the following column, only one of the meet-

ing members is cut away.

The rabbet joint is a simple one to construct, and it's quite strong, too. To ensure adequate strength, be sure to secure the meeting members with nails or screws and glue.

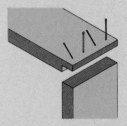

This joint is often used in the construction of inset backs for units such as cabinets and bookshelves (see the sketch below). To make this joint, rabbet each of the framing members, then care-

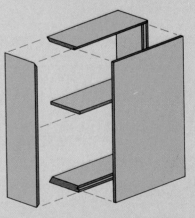

fully measure the distance between the rabbeted openings. Cut the back accordingly. Then use thin screws to secure the back to the unit.

Mortise and Tenon Joints

A particularly strong joint, the mortise and tenon joint is excellent when used for making T joints, right-angle joints, and for joints in the middle of rails. As its name indicates, this joint has two

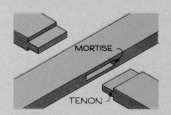

parts—the *mortise,* which is the open part of the joint, and the *tenon,* the part that fits into the mortise.

Make the mortise first, as it is much easier to fit the tenon to the mortise than the other way around. Divide the rail (the part to be mortised) into thirds and carefully mark off the depth and the width of the opening with a sharp pencil.

Next, use a chisel, equal to the width of the mortise, to remove the wood between the pencil marks. You can expedite this job by drilling a series of holes in the rail with an electric drill, a drill press, or even a hand drill. (If you have a drill press, you can purchase a special mortising bit that will drill square holes, believe it or not.) Mark the drill bit with a bit of tape to indicate the desired depth. Now use the chisel to remove the excess wood.

To make the tenon, divide the rail into thirds, mark the required depth, and use a backsaw to remove unwanted wood. If you have a bench or radial saw, the job of removing the wood will be much easier. Use a dado blade and set the blades high enough to remove the outer third of the wood. Reverse the work and remove the lower third, leaving the inner third intact.

To assemble, make a trial fit, and if all is well, apply some white glue to the tenon and insert it into the mortise. If by chance the tenon is too small for the mortise, simply insert hardwood wedges at top and bottom.

Use moderate clamping pressure on the joint until the glue dries overnight. Too much pressure will squeeze out the glue, actually weakening the joint.

Miter Joints

You can join two pieces of wood meeting at a right angle rather elegantly with a miter joint. And it's not a difficult joint to make. All you need is a miter box and a backsaw, or a power saw that you can adjust to cut at a 45 degree angle.

Since the simple miter joint is a surface joint with no shoulders for support, you must reinforce it. The easiest way to do this is with nails and glue (see sketch at the top of the following column). You'll notice that most picture

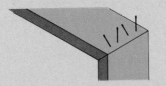

frames are made this way.

However, for cabinet and furniture work, you may use other means of reinforcement. One way is to use a hardwood spline as shown in the drawing. Apply glue to the spline and to the mitered

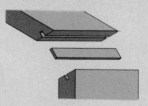

area and clamp as shown until the glue dries.

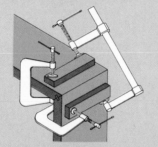

A variation of the long spline uses several short splines—at least three—inserted at opposing angles.

Dowels are a popular method of reinforcing a mitered joint, too. Careful drilling of the holes is necessary to make certain the dowel holes align. Use dowels that are slightly shorter than the holes they are to enter to allow for glue at the bottom. Score or roughen the

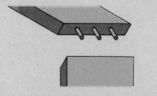

dowels to give the glue a better surface for a strong bond.

Dovetail Joints

The dovetail joint is a sign of good craftsmanship. It's a strong joint especially good for work subject

to heavy loads.

To make the joint, first draw the outline of the pin as shown and

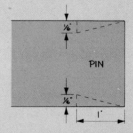

cut away the excess wood with a sharp backsaw. Place the pin over the second piece of wood and draw its outline with a sharp pencil. Make the two side cuts with the backsaw and an additional cut or two to facilitate the next step—chiseling away the excess wood. Then test for fit, apply glue and clamp the pieces until

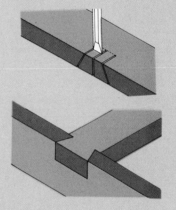

dry. This is the basic way to make most dovetail joints. However, it's much easier to make dovetail joints with a router and dovetail template, especially made for home craftsman use.

Corner Joints

These joints are used for attaching legs to corners for framing. A good technique for joining corners is the three-way joint involving a set of steel braces you can buy. First, insert the bolt into the inside corner of the leg. Then cut slots into the side members, and secure the brace with two screws at each end. Finally, tighten the wing nut.

A variation of the three-way joint uses dowels and a triangular ¾-inch-thick gusset plate for additional reinforcement. To make this joint, first glue the dowels in

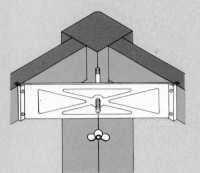

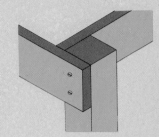

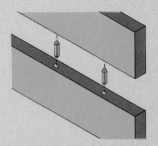

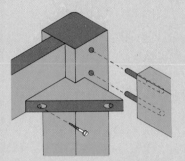

the vertical piece (see sketch). Let them dry completely, then finish the assembly.

A glued miter joint, reinforced with screws and glue, also makes a good corner joint. Make sure the screws do not penetrate the outside surface of the mitered joint.

Probably the strongest of the corner joints is the mortise and tenon (with mitered ends) reinforced with screws (see sketch). The miters on the ends of the tenons allow for a buildup of glue in the mortise, which in turn makes the joint stronger. Make sure that the holes you drill for the screws are not in line with each other.

of being fastened to each other, the butted members are each fastened to the corner post with screws.

Edge-to-Edge Joints

Whenever an extra-wide surface is required, such as a desk top, workbench, or a large storage cabinet, this joint fills the bill. To make it, glue together two or more boards, then hold securely with either bar or pipe clamps. If the boards have a pronounced grain, reverse them side-to-side

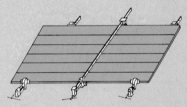

to minimize warping. For additional strength, screw cleats to the underside of the boards.

You also can use hardwood splines to join several boards. Cut a groove the exact width of the spline along the meeting sides of the two boards (see sketch). Cut the grooves slightly deeper than the spline width and in the exact center of the board thickness. The best way to cut such grooves is with a router or a bench saw.

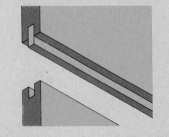

Then assemble with glue and clamps.

Another possibility for joining several boards involves the use of dowels. To make this joint, first

make holes in the boards. You can either use a doweling jig or a drill. If you use a drill, first drive

brads (small finishing nails) into one board and press them against the second board to leave marks for drilling. Make the dowel holes slightly deeper than the dowels. Score the dowels, apply glue, join the two boards together, and clamp with pipe or bar clamps until the glue sets (allow plenty of time).

If you'll be drilling many dowel holes, you may want to use a wood or metal template to ensure accurate spacing.

Box Joints

One joint is so common in the construction of boxes — and drawers — it's called a *box joint*, or a *finger joint because its parts* look like the outstretched fingers of a hand (see sketch). Note that one of the mating pieces must have two end fingers, or one more

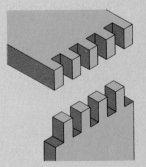

finger than the piece it is to engage. You can make this joint by hand with a backsaw and a small, sharp chisel. However, it is much easier, quicker, and more accurate to make it on a bench saw. Use a dado blade set to the desired width and proper depth of the fingers and mark off the waste area so there will be no mistake as to what you want to cut away.

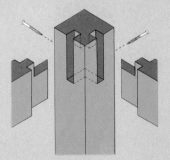

Otherwise, the wood may split. Use flathead screws and countersink the holes.

The simplest corner joint of all is a butt joint for the two horizontal members (see sketch). Instead

SUPPORT SYSTEMS

Any item you construct, no matter how light, must be capable of supporting itself as well as its "payload". Even a simple box has a support system: its sides are self-supporting, each one serving to support and strengthen its neighbor.

How to Attach Things to Walls

Many items, such as shelves and wall-hung cabinets, depend on the wall as part of their support system. However, you can't always drive a nail or insert a screw just anywhere in a wall. For best stability, drive them into the studs of the wall.

Locating studs. One way of locating wall studs is to rap the wall with your knuckles. Listen for a "solid" sound. (Thumps between the studs will sound hollow.) This works fine if you have excellent hearing.

A far easier way is to buy an inexpensive stud finder. Its magnetic needle will respond to hidden nails, indicating the presence of a stud.

Locating one stud does not necessarily mean that the next stud is 16 inches away, though. It should be, but many times it isn't. For example, if the framework of a door or wall falls 20 inches away from the last stud, the builder may have left a 20-inch gap between them. Or, a stud may have been placed midway, leaving 10-inch spaces on either side.

Fastening to hollow-core walls. Quite often, because of physical requirements, you will need to make an installation between studs into a hollow plaster wall.

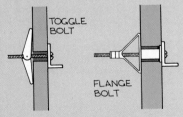

TOGGLE BOLT

FLANGE BOLT

What then? The answer is to use flange or toggle bolts. They distribute their load over a wide area,

and if used in sufficient number and with discretion, they'll hold a fairly heavy load.

Fastening to masonry. Attaching items to a masonry wall is not difficult. if you're working with a brick, concrete, or cinder block wall, use a carbide-tipped drill to make a hole in the mortar. Make the hole deep and wide enough to accept a wall plug. Then insert the screw or bolt to fasten the item in place (see sketch).

Another method of fastening to

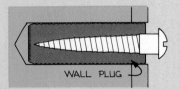

WALL PLUG

masonry walls is to drill a ½-inch hole in the mortar and pound a hardwood dowel into the hole. Bevel the end of the dowel and lightly coat it with grease before driving it in place. Then drill a pilot hole in the middle of the dowel and continue with the fastening.

If by chance you must drill into the brick part of a wall rather than the mortar, don't despair. Again use a carbide-tipped drill, but this time start with a ¼-inch bit, and finish with the larger size desired.

How to Mount Units On a Base

If your project is any type of cabinet, a base is a good idea. A base should provide toe space of at least 3½ inches in height and 2¾ inches in depth. If you plan to mount the unit on casters, you'll automatically get toe space that makes the project convenient.

Box base. This easy-to-build recessed base consists of a four-sided open box installed at the

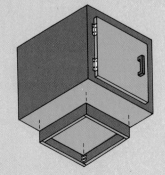

bottom of the cabinet or storage unit. Since appearance is not a factor, you can construct the box with simple butt joints and secure it to the cabinet with steel angle brackets installed along the inside of the base (see sketch).

Leg base. Four short, stubby legs also make a good base. Commercial legs come with their own mounting plate, which is screwed to the bottom of the cabinet before the leg is screwed into place (see sketch). You can also install home-built legs with hanger bolts.

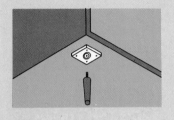

These bolts have a "wood" thread on one end and a coarse "machine" thread on the other end. Drill an undersize hole in the cabinet for the machine end, insert the hanger bolt using pliers and screw the leg into place.

A good source for low-priced legs is a lumberyard that does millwork. Quite often, they'll have a bin full of legs of all sizes that may have slight imperfections or chips which won't affect their serviceability.

How to Mount Shelves

Shelves are a quick and easy way of getting additional storage space in your home, shop, or garage. The best material for shelving is ¾-inch plywood or pine boards—8, 10, 12 inches wide, depending on the items to be stored. To prevent sagging, install a shelf support every 30 inches. And don't use hardboard or chip board, as they tend to bow under heavy loads.

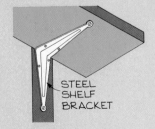

STEEL SHELF BRACKET

Shelf brackets. The easiest way to mount a shelf is by means of steel shelf brackets sold in hardware stores (see sketch). Ask for brackets whose short leg is nearly equal to the *width* of the shelf you plan to install. And always mount the brackets with the *long* leg against the wall. Screw the brackets into the wall and space them about 30 inches apart. For heavy loads, shop around for brackets that have gussets connecting the two legs. Brackets without gussets tend to sway under heavy loads.

Cleats and angle brackets. The narrow space between two walls is an ideal location for shelving. Simply install a pair of cleats at the heights where you want shelves (see sketch). Use cleats that are at least ¾ inch thick and as long as the shelf is wide.

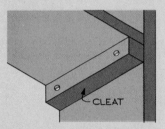

If the walls are of masonry, secure the cleats with so-called steel cut nails (wear goggles when driving these, as they may break off if not struck head-on). Secure the cleats with screws if the walls are of wood, or use flange bolts if they're hollow.

You can also use small steel angle brackets. Mount two under each side of the shelf as shown.

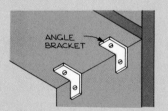

Dowels. Another method of supporting shelves is with dowels. Drill holes equal to the diameter of the dowels, and bore them deep enough to accept at least ½-inch of dowel length. (Make sure both left and right holes are the same height; you might use a level on the shelves to ensure exact mounting.)

Use ¼-inch dowels for light-duty shelves and ⅜-inch dowels for shelves supporting heavy loads. Beveling the dowel ends

will make them easier to insert into the holes. To change shelf spacing, simply drill additional holes.

Dado cuts. This method of supporting shelves has long been a favorite with master cabinetmakers. First, determine the height of the shelf, mark the uprights, and make your cuts. Then cut the shelf to fit.

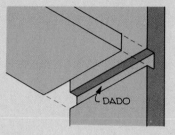

Metal tracks and brackets. You can recess or surface-mount these handy shelf supports. Shelf brackets, specially designed to fit into the track slots, are made to accept 8-, 10-, and 12-inch-wide shelves. Special brackets which adjust to hold shelves at a downward slope also are available and are used to hold dictionaries and reference books.

These tracks and brackets are available in finishes to match the decor of practically any room.

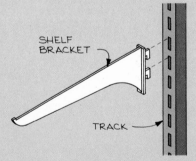

When installing shelves in a cabinet, mount two tracks on each side of the cabinet and use small clips to hold the shelves in place. To change the spacing between shelves, just remove the clips and reposition.

Furring strips. These are especially useful for supporting and erecting shelves in the garage or workshop. Use 2x4s bolted or screwed to the wall and short lengths of 1x4s for shelf supports, as indicated in the drawing. Note that one end is dadoed into the 2x4 (½-inch depth is enough). The

front end of the shelf support bracket is supported by a 1x2 cut at a 45 degree angle at the bottom and engages a cutout called a *bird's mouth* at the top. Toenail

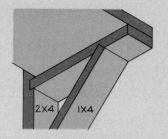

the lower end of the 1x2 into the 2x4. There's no need to nail the upper end, as the weight of the shelf will keep it in place.

Support from above. While most shelves are supported from the bottom, you can also support them from the top. This top support method is especially applicable in basement areas where the joists are exposed. You can nail 2x4s to the joists and fit any type of

project—open shelves, a cabinet, even a work surface between them. If the project to be suspended will run perpendicular to the joists, be careful to plan the length so that it will match the spacing of the joists.

Another way to support shelving from the top is use threaded rods (see sketch above). Choose rods from ¼- to ¾-inch diameter according to the load you'll support. Drill holes in the shelves slightly oversize. To attach the upper end of the rod, drill holes in 2x2 scraps and screw to the joists. Insert the rod and add a nut and washer to the top.

Then install the shelves with a nut and washer on both top and bottom. Tighten the nuts securely to give the shelves as much stability as possible.

HOW TO MAKE DRAWERS

Next to shelves, drawers are the most convenient place for storage. And a drawer is comparatively easy to build. It's just a five-sided box, connected at its corners with the joints previously described.

Types of Drawers

Drawers, no matter how they're made, fall into two general classifications—the flush or recessed type, and the lip type.

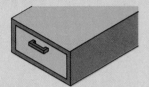

Flush drawers. You must fit this type of drawer carefully to the cabinet opening, with only enough clearance at top and sides to facilitate sliding in and out. In fact, some custom cabinetmakers often will make flush-type drawers with a taper of 1/16 inch from front to back to ensure a good appearance and an easy-sliding fit.

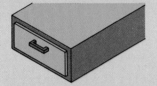

Lipped drawers. These drawers have an oversize front panel that completely covers the drawer opening and so offers much greater leeway in fitting the drawer into its recess.

One way to make a lipped drawer is to rabbet the front panel to the sides and bottom of the drawer, leaving an overlap of ½ inch or so. A simpler way is to screw a false front to the finished drawer front. With this method, if there is any error in construction, the false front will hide it. Attach the drawer front with countersunk flathead screws from the *inside* of the drawer. In addition to the screws, apply white glue between the two pieces.

Construction Details

When making drawers, remember to make the cabinet first, then fit the drawers to the cabinet openings. To make a drawer, first determine its length and cut two pieces of wood to this size and the required width. (The width, of course, will be the height of the finished drawer.)

Draw two parallel lines, equal to the thickness of the drawer back, about ½ inch from the ends

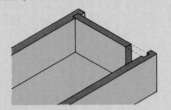

of the two pieces. Cut a dado between these lines to a depth of ¼ inch.

Next, measure the inside distance between the two sides of the drawer opening and cut the drawer back to this measurement. (Allow for clearance and the depth of the dado cuts in the drawer sides.)

For the front of the drawer, plan simple butt joints and cut it to allow a ¼-inch overhang on all sides, if you plan a lip.

You are now ready to partially assemble the drawer. Brush some white glue into the two dado cuts and install the back panel. Use three or four brads at each joint to secure the sides. Next attach the drawer front using glue and brads or screws to secure it to the sides.

A false front nailed or screwed to the existing front from the inside of the drawer will conceal the original brads or screws. If you use brads, countersink them with a nail set.

The bottom of the drawer consists of ¼-inch or thicker plywood, and is nailed to the sides and back of the drawer. For stronger, more elaborate construction, you can use any one of the woodworking joints described earlier in this section.

Drawer Runners and Guides

To ensure that the drawers you build will move in and out without wobbling, you can use any one of

three methods: guides located at each side of the drawer; a central guide placed at the bottom of the drawer; or commercial metal tracks mounted on the sides of the cabinet with nylon wheels on the drawer sides. These come in lengths to fit most drawers and are especially good for heavy loads. Select them before you build the drawer in order to plan the clearance space.

The simplest guide consists of two narrow lengths of wood secured to each side of the drawer, spaced an inch apart (see sketch). Another strip of wood, mounted on each side of the

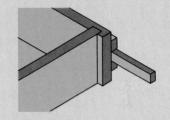

drawer opening, fits the "track" mounted on the drawer sides. To ease operation, apply paste wax to all touching surfaces.

For guides at the bottom of the drawer, mount lengths of wood on the cabinet and engage the two strips of wood on the bottom of the drawer.

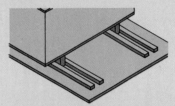

If you're planning to incorporate runners and guides in the drawers, make allowances before starting work. A clearance of ½-inch is required for guides mounted at the sides of the drawers, and 1 inch for center-mounted guides. Regardless of what type of drawer guides you use, make sure you install them accurately.

You can even make easy-sliding drawers without guides or runners by installing plastic glides in the drawer openings so the bottom of the drawer will bear against plastic instead of wood. Steel thumbtacks also ease drawer movement. But don't forget to apply wax to the bottom bearing surfaces of the drawer.

HOW TO INSTALL CABINET DOORS

Except for shelves, tables, and chairs, nearly every piece of furniture you build will have some sort of door. All doors require hinges or tracks, and handles for opening and closing. Here are the basics.

Construction Pointers

To prevent warping, cabinet doors should be at least ½ inch thick. However, you can use a ¼-inch panel, providing you frame it with ½-inch wood, somewhat like a picture frame.

If you plan to laminate a door panel with plastic, use the thin grade laminate especially made for vertical surfaces. The heavy grade, made for countertops, may cause the cabinet to warp.

Sliding Doors

Sliding doors are easier to fit and install than swinging doors, and, as a rule, are of much lighter stock than conventional doors. Track for sliding doors can be aluminum or plastic (left sketch), or it can consist of grooves cut into the top and bottom of the framework (right sketch).

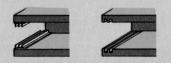

Of course, you must cut these grooves before assembly. Make the upper grooves about twice as deep as the bottom ones so you can lift up, then lower the door into place. The doors should be flush with the bottom shelf surface when it's touching the top of the upper groove.

To ease sliding, apply wax or a silicone spray to the grooves. If you're planning to use handles, recess them into the door so there will be no interference when the doors bypass each other.

Hinged Doors

Flush-type hinged doors that recess within the framing require clearance all around to prevent binding. To install a flush-type door, make a dry fit, and if the door fits, insert small wedges at all sides to hold it in place and ensure clearance until the hinges have been completely installed.

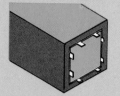

Then place the hinge against the door—if it's an exterior mounting—and mark the hinge holes with an awl. Drill pilot holes and install the hinges. Use this same procedure if you have an interior mounting job.

With hinges that are partly concealed—half on the inside of the door and half on the frame—mount the hinges on the door first, set the door in place, and mark the location of the hinge on the frame or door jamb. This method is much easier than trying to fit an already-mounted hinge to the blind or interior part of the door.

Types of hinges. There are literally dozens of types of hinges to choose from. Following are a few of the more common varieties.

As a general rule, you should mortise hinges into cabinets so they are flush with the work. However, always surface mount decorative hinges, such as colonial, rustic, and ornamental hinges.

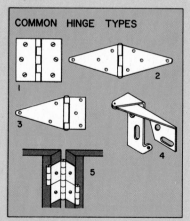

COMMON HINGE TYPES

(1) *Butt hinges* are the type you're probably most familiar with. Use them for either right- or left-hand doors. The larger sizes have re-

movable pins to facilitate taking off the door; the smaller sizes don't. For long cabinet doors or lids. use a piano hinge (a long butt hinge) rather than several smaller ones. (2, 3) The *strap hinge* and the *T hinge* are used for extra-heavy doors. There's no need to mortise these hinges, as they are strictly functional.

(4) *Pivot hinges*, also called knife hinges, are available in different shapes and are especially good for use on ¾-inch plywood doors. All shapes present a very unobtrusive appearance.

(5) *Double-acting hinges* allow a door to be swung from either direction.

Self-closing hinges operate by means of a spring concealed within the barrel of the hinge. Another type, used on kitchen cabinets, has no spring, yet closes the door with a positive snapping action. Its secret is a square shoulder next to the pin.

Special-purpose hinges are available with offset leaves (so the door will overlap the framing); hinges with knuckles (for quick door removal); ball-bearing hinges lubricated for life (for extra-heavy doors); hinges that will automatically raise a door when it is opened (so that it will clear a carpet on the far side of the door); burglar-resistant hinges (with pins that can't be removed when they're on the outside); and hinges that allow a door to be swung back far enough so that the full width of the doorway can be utilized.

Door catches and handles. In addition to hinges, you will need hardware to keep the doors closed and to lock them. For cabinet work, your best hardware bets are spring-loaded or magnetic catches.

Spring-loaded catches come with single and double rollers and are ideal for lipped doors, flush doors, double doors, and shelves. These catches are adjustable.

Install magnetic catches so there is physical contact between the magnet in the frame and the "keeper" on the door.

A handle of some type is required for all drawers and doors. Handles can be surface-mounted or recessed flush with the drawer or door. Sliding doors always use recessed handles so the doors can bypass each other.

THE HARDWARE YOU'LL NEED

For any sort of fastening work, you will need nails, screws, and bolts, as well as glues and cements.

Nails, Screws, and Bolts

These most common of all fastening materials are available in diverse widths and lengths, and in steel, brass, aluminum, copper, and even stainless steel.

Nails. Nails are sold by the penny—which has nothing to do with their cost. The "penny," (abbreviated *d*) refers to the size. The chart shows a box nail marked in the penny size designations as well as actual lengths in inches.

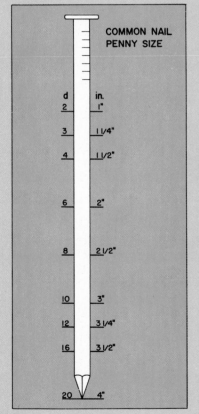

COMMON NAIL PENNY SIZE

d	in.
2	1"
3	1 1/4"
4	1 1/2"
6	2"
8	2 1/2"
10	3"
12	3 1/4"
16	3 1/2"
20	4"

Use common nails for general-purpose work; finish and casing nails for trim or cabinetwork; and brads for attaching molding to walls and furniture.

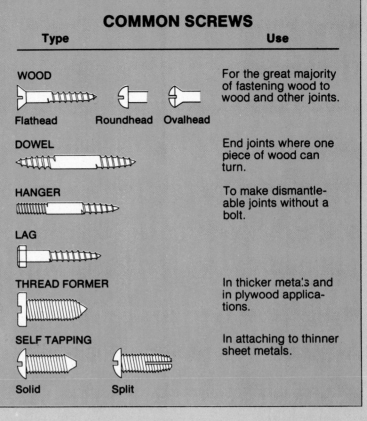

COMMON SCREWS

Type	Use
WOOD — Flathead, Roundhead, Ovalhead	For the great majority of fastening wood to wood and other joints.
DOWEL	End joints where one piece of wood can turn.
HANGER	To make dismantle-able joints without a bolt.
LAG	
THREAD FORMER	In thicker metals and in plywood applications.
SELF TAPPING — Solid, Split	In attaching to thinner sheet metals.

Finishing

Casing

Brad

Screws. Screws are sold by length and diameter. The diameter is indicated by a number, from 1 to 16. The thicker the screw shank, the larger the number. The drawing shows some of the most popular types of screws.

Always drill a pilot hole when inserting a screw into hardwood. And always drill a clearance hole in the leading piece of wood when screwing two pieces of wood together. Without a clearance hole, the leading piece tends to "hang up," preventing a tight fit between the two.

Bolts. You can also fasten wood together with bolts, but only if there is access to the back for the required washer and nut. A bolted joint is stronger than a screwed joint, as the bolt diameter is generally thicker than the comparable screw, and also because the wrench used to tighten the nut can apply much more force than a screwdriver in a screw slot.

Glues and Cements

While not "hardware" as such, glue is an important adjunct to any fastening job. The so-called white glue is excellent for use with wood, and only moderate clamping pressure is required. When dry, it is crystal clear. However, it's not waterproof so don't use it for work subject to excessive dampness—and of course, never for outdoor use. Use the two-tube epoxy "glue" for joints that must be waterproof.

Plastic resin glue, a powder that you mix with water to a creamy consistency, is highly water resistant.

Contact cement provides an excellent bond between wood and wood, and wood and plastic. When working with contact cement, remember that it dries instantly and position your surfaces

COMMON BOLTS

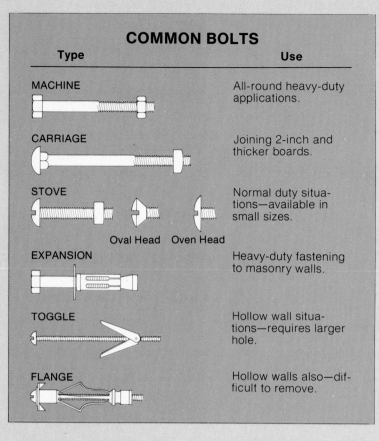

Type	Use
MACHINE	All-round heavy-duty applications.
CARRIAGE	Joining 2-inch and thicker boards.
STOVE — Oval Head, Oven Head	Normal duty situations—available in small sizes.
EXPANSION	Heavy-duty fastening to masonry walls.
TOGGLE	Hollow wall situations—requires larger hole.
FLANGE	Hollow walls also—difficult to remove.

The plate type caster is merely screwed to the bottom by four screws that pass through holes in the plate. They are not height adjustable unless, of course, you use shims.

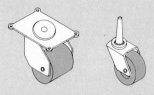

All casters use ball bearings as part of the plate assembly to facilitate swiveling. For extra-heavy usages, purchase casters with ball-bearing wheels as well.

The wheels on casters are of two types—plastic or rubber. Use casters with plastic wheels if the project is to be rolled on a soft surface such as a rug; rubber wheeled casters are best on hard concrete, vinyl, or hardwood. It's a good idea to use graphite to lubricate the wheels and their bearings, as oil tends to pick up dust and dirt.

To prevent a caster-equipped unit from rolling, get locking casters. A small lever on the outside of the wheel locks a "brake." Brakes on only two of the four casters on a unit are sufficient.

When to Use What Glue

Type	Use
White glue (No mixing)	Paper, cloth, wood
Epoxy (requires mixing)	Wood, metal, stone (waterproof)
Plastic resin (requires mixing)	Wood to wood (water resistant)
Contact cement (no mixing)	Wood to wood or plastic (waterproof)
Waterproof glue (requires mixing)	Wood to wood (waterproof)

together exactly as you want them. You won't get a second chance.

True waterproof glue comes in two containers; one holds a liquid resin, the other a powder catalyst. When dry, this glue is absolutely waterproof and can be safely used for garden equipment and all outdoor projects and furniture.

Glides and Casters

The intended use determines whether a piece of furniture needs a caster or a glide. If you don't plan to move it frequently, use a glide; otherwise, a caster is the best choice.

Glides come in many sizes, determined by the glide area touching the floor, and with steel or plastic bottoms. The simple nail-on glides aren't height adjustable but you can adjust screw glides by screwing the glide in or out to prevent wobbling if the floor is uneven, or if by some chance, the project does not have an even base.

Casters are made in two styles—stem type (only the stem type is adjustable) and plate type (at left in sketch). The stem type requires a hole to be drilled into the leg or base of the cabinet or furniture. This hole accepts a sleeve that in turn accepts the stem of the caster.

Miscellaneous Hardware

There are many types of hardware that can come in handy when you're constructing storage bins, cabinets, chests, shelves, and other projects.

Following are some you may need from time to time: corrugated fasteners connect two boards or mend splits in wood; angle irons reinforce corners; flat and T plates also reinforce work; masonry nails secure work to concrete or brick walls; steel plates with a threaded center are used for attaching legs to cabinets; screw eyes and cup hooks allow for hanging items inside storage units; and lag screw plugs made of lead or plastic secure furring strips or shelf brackets to masonry walls.

You'll be wise to stock your workshop with most of these items in a couple of sizes. That way, you won't have to make a special trip when they're needed.

FINISHING TECHNIQUES

Finishing is your final job before you can step back and admire your work. Before starting, make sure that all nails are flush or countersunk and filled, all flathead screws are flush with the surface, all cracks are filled, and all surfaces are sanded and cleaned.

Hardboard and Chip Board

If the unit you have built is made of hardboard, about the only finish you can apply to it is paint. No preparation is needed except to remove any oil or dirt. Inasmuch as hardboard is brown—the tempered type is a darker brown—you'll need to apply at least two coats of paint if you want the final finish to be a light color.

Hardboard will accept latex or alkyd paints equally well. Between coats, let dry overnight and then sand lightly.

You also can paint chip board, flake board, and particle board, but because of their slightly rougher texture you should apply a "filler" coat of shellac first, then proceed with painting.

Plywood

Because of its comparatively low cost, fir plywood is used extensively for building projects. However, the hard and soft growth patterns in the wood will show through unless a sealer is used before painting or finishing with varnish or lacquer.

After sealing, sand lightly and finish with at least two coats of paint, varnish, or lacquer. The final step for varnish or lacquer work consists of an application of paste wax applied with fine steel wool and polishing with terry cloth or any other coarse-textured cloth.

Plywood has a pronounced end grain due to its layered construction. If your project will be on display, it's best to hide the end grain, and there are several ways to do this.

A mitered joint is the obvious solution, as then the end grain is hidden within the joint. Another solution is wood veneer tape (see sketch). This tape comes in rolls and is really walnut, oak, mahogany, or a similar wood in a very thin strip about ¾ inch wide. Either glue it or use contact cement, applying the cement to the tape and to the plywood edges. When the cement has lost its gloss, carefully align the tape and press over the plywood edge.

You also can use molding to cover the edges. It has the additional advantage of making a decorative edge requiring no further treatment.

Metal molding is another option, especially useful for edges which are subject to wear and abuse.

A rabbet joint will also hide end grain. Make the rabbet deep enough so that only the last ply is uncut.

Other Woods

If your project is constructed of a fine wood, a more elaborate finishing technique is needed.

Sanding. You can do this by hand or with a power sander. A power belt sander is fine for initial sanding, but always do the final sanding with an orbital or straight line finishing sander—or with fine sandpaper.

Filling and staining. Open grain woods such as oak, chestnut, walnut, ash, and mahogany require a filler to close their pores. Apply the filler with a brush or rag, wiping across the grain. After 10 or 15 minutes, remove the excess filler with a coarse cloth.

If a stain is called for, let the wood dry for 24 hours before application. A stain applied over a filler that has not dried will show up as a "hot" spot.

Sealing. A sealer, as its name implies, is used to seal the stains and filler from the subsequent finishing coats.

One of the best sealers is shellac. One advantage of using shellac is that it prevents the stain from bleeding. Thin the shellac with alcohol to the consistency of light cream; as it comes in the can, it's much too thick for use as a sealer. You can also use ready-mixed stains combined with a sealer.

Finishes. *Varnish,* the traditional finish for wood, is available in many types and colors.

To prepare a piece for varnish, sand it lightly, wipe off the dust with a turpentine-dampened rag, and apply the varnish with long, flowing strokes. Do not brush out the varnish as you would paint. And don't use varnish during humid weather. To make sure the varnish will flow evenly, place the can in warm water.

Varnish requires at least two coats, with a minimum of 24 hours drying time. Sand lightly between coats. After the second or third coat has dried for at least a week, rub down with steel wool and paste wax. Polish with a rough cloth.

Shellac, too, will yield super results. It's fairly easy to work with and it dries dust free in a half-hour. You can apply the second coat within two hours. Sanding is not required between coats, as the second coat tends to partially dissolve and melt into the first one.

One disadvantage of shellac is that it shows a ring if a liquor-stained glass is placed on a shellac-finished surface. Also, shellac sometimes tends to crack if exposed to dampness.

Polyurethane is a tough synthetic varnish that resists abrasion, alcohol, and fruit stains. It's great for floors, furniture, walls, and woodwork. To apply polyurethane the surface must be clean, dry, and free of grease, oil, and wax. Don't apply a polyurethane finish over previously shellacked or lacquered surfaces. Allow at least 12 hours drying time for each coat, and clean your brushes with mineral spirits or turpentine.

Lacquer is a fast-drying finish you can apply by spray or brush. For spraying, thin lacquer only with lacquer thinner. *Never use turpentine or mineral spirits.*

To brush lacquer, always use a brush that has *never* been used to apply paint.

And never apply lacquer over a painted surface, as the lacquer will lift the paint. As with shellac, sanding between coats is not necessary.

HOW TO WATERPROOF A BASEMENT

Water is the scourge of finished basements. Even a small amount of it can ruin the fruits of your labor. Be sure to check your basement walls and floor for tell-tale water stains or excessive humidity before starting any remodeling project.

Basement dampness comes from one of three sources: condensation, seepage, or leaks.

Condensation/ Seepage

Even a well-sealed basement may collect extra moisture through condensation. When warm, moist air meets the cooler basement walls and floors, dampness may form. Solve this problem by making sure your clothes dryer is properly vented and that your basement has good air circulation. You may need a dehumidifier, too.

Seepage is caused by water forcing its way through pores in the foundation walls. Often, it's hard to tell seepage from condensation. If in doubt, tape a small mirror to your basement wall for a day or so. If moisture has *not* condensed on the mirror, yet the walls still feel damp, seepage is your problem.

To solve a seepage problem, check gutters and downspouts to be sure they are free-flowing. Then, make sure the ground around your foundation slopes *away* from your basement walls . . . enough that water drains at least six feet away from the foundation during a rain.

To treat seepage on the inside of your walls, apply one of the epoxy-base compounds. Or, trowel on a waterproof cement.

NOTE: If the water table is higher than your basement floor and threatens to break the slab, you may have to break away a section of the floor around the walls and install drain tiles. Or, the solution may be to excavate around the foundation, applying a waterproof barrier of tar or vinyl

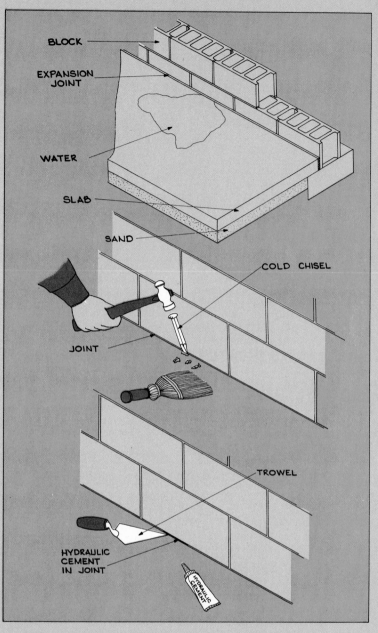

sheeting to the wall and laying tiles along the footing.

Leaks

Caused by cracks in the foundation walls or basement floor, leaks are usually a relatively minor problem that comes with normal settling. NOTE: Cracks may also be the first indication of a structural fault—watch for changes in them over a long period of time.

The same procedures previously described for keeping water away from the exterior walls will help prevent small leaks from becoming big problems. For best results, also patch cracks and leaks from the inside using hydraulic cement or epoxy.

When patching a leak (see top sketch), first enlarge the crack or hole using a cold chisel (middle sketch). Make a dovetail shape with the chisel to help hold the patch, then clean debris away. Apply hydraulic cement or epoxy compound and smooth patch with a trowel (bottom sketch).

HOW TO BUILD A PARTITION WALL

Sooner or later, you'll probably want to build a partition wall as part of a large-scale remodeling job, such as finishing your basement or dividing a room. And when you do, it will help to know the basics of wall construction before you start planning where and how to build your new wall.

Placement of Wall

When you lay out the plans for your new wall, take a moment to notice the direction of the ceiling joists. Ideally, the partition should run perpendicular to the joists. But, if you must construct parallel to the joists, try to plan your dimensions to place the wall directly under a joist.

If for some reason you have to locate the partition parallel to — but not directly beneath — a joist, you can anchor the top plate to a series of nailers cut to fit between the surrounding joists and nailed into place (see top sketch for various position possibilities).

Next, mark the location of the wall, recruiting someone to help snap chalk lines. Snap the location of the top plate first; then, use a plumb line to transfer the ceiling lines to the floor. Snap a line for location of sole plate.

Now, you're ready to install the wall. There are two methods to use . . . choose the one you judge best for your situation.

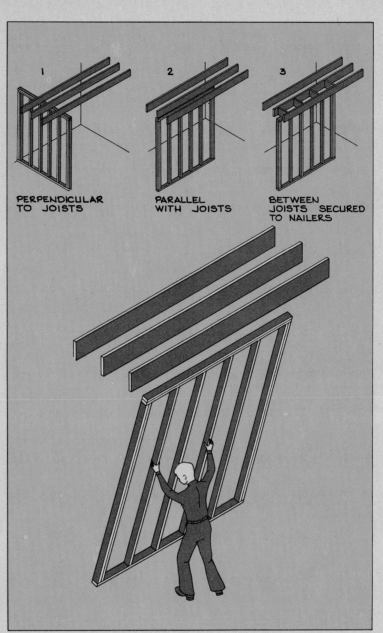

PERPENDICULAR TO JOISTS

PARALLEL WITH JOISTS

BETWEEN JOISTS SECURED TO NAILERS

Pre-Assembly Method

Sometimes it's easiest to build the partition flat on the floor, then raise it into position as a unit. To do this, first cut 2x4 sole plate and top plates the exact length of the wall, then cut your studs to the correct height.

Next, assemble your wall. Working on the floor where you have room, build the framework by spiking through the top and bottom plates into the ends of 2x4 studs, positioned 16 inches on center. Measure the 16-inch intervals from a point ¾ inch in from

the end that will tie to an existing wall. If studs are warped, turn them so the bow is in one direction. Nail double studs into each corner for strength.

NOTE: To ensure a snug fit when you put up the partition wall, be sure to make your measurements carefully.

Erect the wall by positioning the bottom plate on the chalk line, and slipping the top plate into position (see sketch). When partition is square, nail it to the joists and into the sidewalls.

Build-As-You-Go Method

Start by snapping chalk lines for the correct location of the top and sole plates. Cut the plates to size. Before installing, mark stud placement on the top and sole plates simultaneously, measuring 16-inch centers. Then nail the top and sole plates into position. Using the previously made markings, nail studs to the top and sole plates. Again, make double-stud corners for strength.

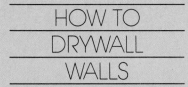

HOW TO DRYWALL WALLS

Drywall is a favorite wall covering because it's easy to work with — and economical, too. Use it on a new stud wall as the base surface for paint, wallpaper, or any other "finish" wall covering. Or install drywall over existing walls to improve sound insulation, cover battered plaster, or hide masonry walls. NOTE: Place insulation between studs or furring strips before installing drywall to cut fuel costs and to provide an excellent vapor barrier.

Furring How-To

When you don't have existing studs or a smooth, even wall surface, it's best to install a framework of furring strips before mounting drywall. Starting from one corner, mark vertical chalk lines on the wall every 16 inches. On a masonry wall, treat the surface with a waterproof sealant that will bond satisfactorily to your furring strip adhesive. Using 1x2 furring strips, cut two long pieces to span the wall horizontally at top and bottom. Then cut a series of framing strips to fit vertically in corners and centered on each chalk line.

Use panel adhesive or nails to attach the strips. Install the long horizontal top and bottom strips first. If using panel adhesive, apply a bead of adhesive along the wall. Press the furring strip against the adhesive for an instant, remove it for about ten minutes, then reapply. Mount the vertical strips the same way until your furring framework is completed. Use shims to even out low spots in the frame.

Installing the Drywall

Starting at one end of the wall, nail sheets of drywall vertically to studs or furring strips. Use a square and rule to make sure the first panel is perfectly square. Nailing the drywall every seven inches with ring-shank nails, install each panel. Keep nails roughly ⅜ inch from the border

HAMMER DIMPLE

on all panels; recess each nail slightly without breaking the face paper (see detail in top sketch).

If you have to cut off a portion of a panel, first score the front face paper with a sharp utility knife—deep enough to cut

through to the core (see top sketch). Break the material by snapping it away from the score over a length of ½-inch dowel or a board, and finish the separation process by slicing through the back layer of paper. With a keyhole saw, cut any openings for electrical boxes or other single obstructions before you install the panels. Butt the panels up to window and door openings.

Filling Joints

Using a four-inch putty knife, spread joint compound in a uniform swath where drywall panels meet. Press two-inch-wide perforated tape into the joint; start at the top, holding the knife at a 45-degree angle (see detail in bottom sketch on previous page). Then apply a thin layer of compound over the tape (see bottom sketch). Also fill each nail dimple.

When the compound is dry—usually overnight—add another coat of compound to the tape, feathering it out about six inches with a special drywall trowel. Give the nailheads a second treatment, too.

As soon as this application dries, use a wet sponge to smooth joints. Let dry. Follow with another coat of compound, if necessary. When dry, sponge smooth (see sketch at right).

Filling Joints at Corners

Outside corners need reinforcement to withstand occasional blows from furniture or carried objects. The solution is metal edging, available in different forms. One type has paper flanges that are embedded in joint compound. Another type is an all-metal bead (see sketch) that you nail every five inches through the drywall into the wood furring or studs beneath.

To install the paper flange variety, coat the corner with joint compound and position the edging. Cover it with more compound, feathering about three inches on each side. Allow to dry overnight; apply a second coat. Sponge smooth when dry.

To install the metal bead type, nail into position as described above. Then follow with two coats of joint compound, sponging and letting dry.

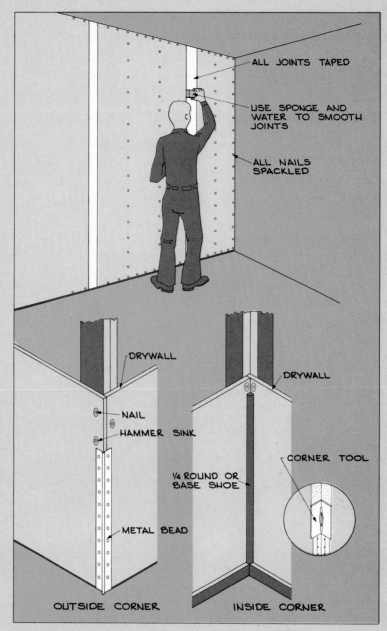

ALL JOINTS TAPED

USE SPONGE AND WATER TO SMOOTH JOINTS

ALL NAILS SPACKLED

DRYWALL

DRYWALL

NAIL

HAMMER SINK

¼ ROUND OR BASE SHOE

CORNER TOOL

METAL BEAD

OUTSIDE CORNER

INSIDE CORNER

Inside corners require a different joint-covering technique. Again, there's more than one way to do the job right. One way is simply to cover the joint with a length of quarter-round or base shoe nailed through the drywall into the furring or stud beneath (see sketch).

A second way to cover an inside joint is with perforated tape and joint compound. First, apply compound to the joint, spreading it out approximately 1½ inches on each side. Cut the tape to length, crease it down the middle, and press it into the corner firmly enough to force compound through the perforations. Feather the edge out past the tape; allow to dry. Follow with a second coat of compound, applying it with a special inside corner tool (see sketch). Allow to dry and follow with a third coat. When dry, sponge smooth.

After drywall installation is complete, dust entire wall. Apply a special primer-sealer before painting or papering.

HOW TO PANEL WALLS

Surface and Panel Preparation

On new walls with exposed studs, no special preparation is necessary. You can nail or glue paneling to the studs, unless you live in one of the few states that requires drywall underneath.

If you're covering existing walls, make sure they're free of flaking paint or loose wallpaper. On even surfaces, nail or glue paneling onto the old wall.

To prepare the paneling, stack the panels in the room to be walled two days ahead of installation. Lay them on some 2x4s so air can circulate and to keep panels off the floor.

Furring How-To

While panels adjust to the room, install furring strips over uneven walls or basement masonry. Lay out the furring as described on page 88. If desired, use horizontal furring as shown at right. In sub-grade basements, add moisture-proof insulation between furring strips; for thicker insulation, use 2x4s as furring.

Before installing the furring, cut and fit a piece of paneling for a corner to check for plumb (it may be far enough off that the trimmed panel may not extend a full four feet from the corner).

Plumb the panel with a level (see sketch). If the fit in the corner leaves a gap of less than ½ inch, don't worry (molding will cover it). If there's more of a gap, trim the panel to fit accordingly. Use the edge of the panel to mark the "start" location of furring strips, then proceed to install all furring.

If your walls are irregular, use an alternate furring procedure. Attach vertical 1x2s to the wall at four-foot centers, measuring from the start-strip position that is described above. Then nail 1x2s horizontally on top of the verticals at the top and bottom of the wall and at 16-inch centers in between. Nail short 1x2 pieces onto the verticals to fill the spaces be-

tween the horizontals. Shim with wood wedges as necessary to achieve an even surface.

Panel Installation

Stand panels against the wall, arranging so colors and grains flow together smoothly. Number in order. Cut panels to proper height, less ¼ inch for easy handling. Make cutouts for outlet boxes and other obstructions with a keyhole saw (see sketch).

To nail the panels in place, use one-inch color-matched nails over the furring, or 1½-inch nails over old walls.

To glue, run beads of panel ad-

hesive along furring strips. Or, if you're installing paneling flush against the wall, snap chalk lines every four feet to indicate junctions. Bead adhesive inside vertical chalk lines and ½ inch from edge along top and bottom. Follow with two beads of adhesive forming a giant "X" across the entire area.

Press panel against the adhesive; partially drive one nail through the top of it into the wall or furring strip. Pull the bottom of the panel away from the wall about eight inches and prop it there with a block of wood until adhesive gets tacky; then replace panel.

HOW TO FINISH A CEILING

New ceilings aren't as much work as they used to be. Today, attractive kits and simplified suspended ceiling systems make installation easy. Whatever type of ceiling you select, be sure to check the manufacturer's specifications and read accompanying instructions thoroughly before starting on your project.

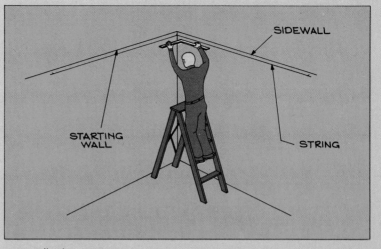

Drywall

If you're planning to paint, wallpaper, or plaster your new ceiling, drywall makes a good base to work from. Nail panels perpendicular to the joists, disguising joints between the panels with perforated tape and joint compound (see instructions on page 88).

You can nail drywall to open joists or over an existing ceiling if the surface is flat and true. If the existing ceiling is uneven, install a series of 1x3 furring strips nailed perpendicular to the joists and shimmed to eliminate low spots. NOTE: Drywall is heavy and difficult to handle for ceiling jobs. Even if you have a helper or two, it's a good idea to use a couple of "T-braces" made from 2x4s and 1x4 crosspieces to help prop the panels during installation.

Ceiling Tiles

A square-tile ceiling is easy to install if your existing ceiling is free of protruding pipes, heating ducts, or major irregularities. The tiles—usually 12 inches square—are either glued or stapled in place.

Measure your ceiling carefully to determine how many tiles you'll need. Also figure the size of your border tiles on all four sides (they should be as even as possible on opposite sides).

Glue tiles directly to drywall or an existing plaster ceiling if the surface is strong, clean, and smooth. If you're installing tiles over exposed joists, put up 1x2 or 1x3 wood furring strips nailed perpendicular to the joists. Nail the first strip into place butted against the wall's edge. Follow with a second strip centered on a mark matching the width of the first row of tiles. From that point on, nail furring at 12-inch centers, butting the last strip against the opposite wall's edge.

Squaring the Room

No matter what type of ceiling you install—either square tiles stapled directly to wood furring or any of the new suspended ceiling panels—you'll want to "square the room" first to achieve professional results.

Start by fastening a string from the starting wall to the opposite wall at a distance away from the sidewall equal to the width of your first border tile. Attach a second string perpendicular to the first from sidewall to sidewall . . . again, positioned according to the size of the first border panel (see sketch). Using a square, adjust the strings until they form an exact 90-degree angle. Cut your first tile and fit it exactly, using the string as a guide. Be sure to cut each of the tiles in your border rows carefully—again, using the string as a guide. This will compensate for the unevenness that characterizes most walls.

Installing Ceiling Tiles

Starting in the corner where your guide strings converge, glue or staple each tile into place. If you're gluing the tiles, use the adhesive recommended by the manufacturer. Press tile into place and put a couple of staples into the flanges to hold the tile until the glue sets. If you're stapling the tiles, drive the staples through the flanges into the furring strips—one staple at each corner.

Proceed to tile along both walls, forming an "L." Then use full-size tiles to fill in between.

Suspended Ceilings

Because of its ease of installation and attractiveness, a suspended ceiling is a good choice in almost any situation . . . particularly when you have heating ducts, plumbing, or electrical conduit to conceal. Various systems are available, with ceiling tiles in 1x1—, 1x4—, or 2x4-foot sizes. Some varieties offer grooves that fit into cross tees and lock into their metal gridwork frame. Other types just pop into place. With either kind you have the advantage of easy tile replacement and quick access to pipes or wiring.

To install your ceiling, first decide on the new ceiling height. Plan on lowering the existing ceiling at least 3½ inches—or more if you like. Then snap level chalk line along the room's walls at the height you select.

Attach the metal angle molding all around the room, lining up the bottom leg of the "angle" with the chalk line (see top sketch on next page). Butt ends of the molding pieces and miter them at the corners of the room. NOTE: if attaching the angle molding to masonry wall, use an adhesive.

Next, locate your ceiling joists if they're not exposed, determin-

HOW TO FINISH A CEILING

(continued)

ing which direction they run (install the main runners at right angles to the joists). Determine the location of the main runners according to the manufacturer's specifications and install eye-screws in the joists at proper locations.

Follow by installing the wire hangers used to support the main runners (see sketch). Carefully position a string beneath every row of hangers to determine the correct height of the main runners (usually 1¾ inches above the bottom edge of the metal angle molding) and bend each wire hanger at a right angle where it touches the string.

Working from the starting wall, butt the open end of a main runner to the wall and attach the hanging wires through holes at the top of the runner. Secure by twisting the wire with pliers. Repeat until all main runners are installed.

Calculate the size of all border tiles. Here, it's best to follow the manufacturer's directions for determining border size.

Starting in one corner of the room, install two strings to "square the room" (follow the instructions for "squaring the room" on page 91). Cut the first tile to size and install it, making doubly sure that it's square, since all other tiles line up from it.

Now you'll want to take careful note of the instructions for your style of ceiling. If you're installing a system in which the tiles are just "dropped" into place (see sketch), the manufacturer probably calls for you to install the entire system of cross tees at this time. For a system that uses interlocking tiles, you'll install the cross tees as you go. Follow the instructions as given.

Proceed to tile the ceiling. When you get to the ends or the sides, cut border tiles to size. If necessary, install small wall springs to push the rows of tiles together (again, see instructions for ceiling).

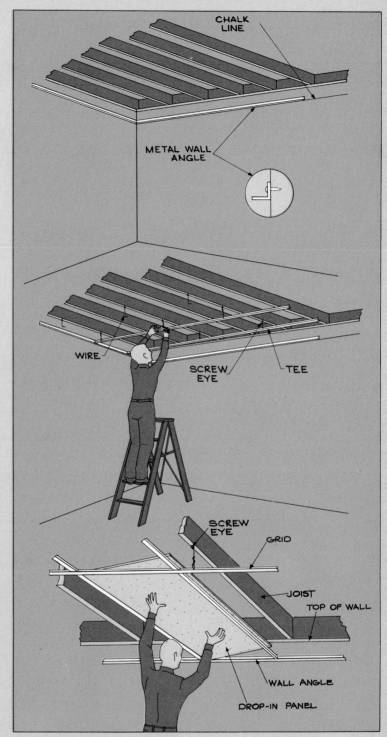

A note about lighting. One of the real advantages of a suspended ceiling system is the ease with which you can install overhead lighting. Many manufacturers offer lighting fixtures designed to drop right into their ceiling supports. Once you've decided where you want to locate your fixtures, install a junction box for each one. Then substitute lighting panels for ceiling panels.

HOW TO LAY RESILIENT FLOORING

For an average-size room, laying a new vinyl floor is just an afternoon's project. Follow these instructions and beautiful results will be yours.

TILES—Getting Ready

Although new vinyl tiles are versatile enough to be laid over old tiles, wood floors, and concrete, the existing floor must be in good condition and free of oil, wax, and grease. And you must reglue any loose tiles. If you're dealing with a wood floor, you'll need to plane or sand high spots. A concrete floor with a moisture problem requires moistureproofing and a new subflooring of plywood or particleboard.

Before getting started, read the instructions accompanying your new tile for suggestions. And don't forget to remove the shoe molding before you begin.

Laying Out the Floor

Use a chalk line to strike two intersecting guidelines, each connecting the midpoints on opposite sides of the floor. Temporarily lay one tile at the junction of the chalk lines, fitting one corner squarely at the intersection of the two lines.

Then, form two rows of loose tiles into an "L" that extends to the walls. If the space for the last row of tiles at one or both walls measures less than half the width of a tile, back up the entire "L" half a tile's width and snap new chalk lines.

Installing the Tile

You can purchase resilient vinyl tile with or without adhesive backing. If you choose to apply adhesive, follow the manufacturer's recommendations for the type of adhesive that will work best for you.

With a notched spreader, and working from a corner of the room, lay down enough adhesive to cover one-fourth of the floor (see top sketch). Re-lay the "L"

(continued)

HOW TO LAY RESILIENT FLOORING

(continued)

permanently; then, fill in the area between with tiles (see middle sketch). Butt each new tile against its neighbor, then *lower* it — don't slide it — into place. Complete the entire floor this way.

If you need to trim tiles for a row that butts against a wall, temporarily position the tile to be trimmed directly over another in the next-to-the-last row (see bottom sketch on previous page). Place a second tile flush against the wall, overlapping the first tile. With the top tile as a guide, score the tile underneath with a sharp knife. The piece you trim off will fit the space you want to fill.

After you complete the entire floor, replace the shoe molding. Nail it to the wall.

SHEET FLOORING— Getting Ready

Prepare your floor's surface so that it's free of dirt, grease, wax, and oil. NOTE: Resilient sheet flooring conforms to irregularities of surface beneath it. For that reason, it's best to install vinyl sheets directly over the subflooring, rather than over the existing tile or hardwood floor.

Laying Out the Floor

Vinyl roll flooring (also called ''cushioned'' vinyl) most often comes in 12-foot-wide rolls. So if your room is wider than 12 feet, you'll have to join two rolls.

When laying out your floor, it's best to do the preliminary work in a large room close to the room you're flooring. First, roll out the flooring in the neighboring room so the vinyl will reach room temperature. Then remove the shoe molding in the room to be floored.

Determine which wall is the longest and straightest (this will be the ''starting wall'' when you roll out flooring). Choose one edge of the vinyl to correspond to starting wall and label it.

Next, transfer the measure-

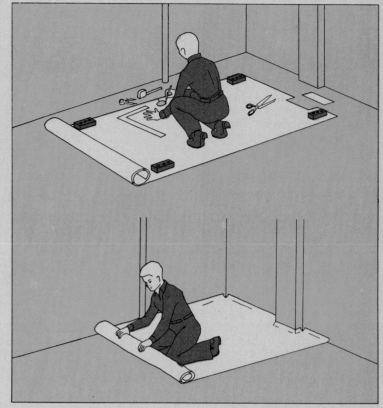

ments of the old wall to the vinyl. If you have to make a seam, temporarily overlap two 12-foot strips so that the patterns match. Draw a line on the bottom sheet (use the edge of the top sheet as a guide) and tape the two together so they don't move while you make other measurements and marks. Also add a few crosshatch marks on both sheets for re-alignment after you transfer the vinyl into the room to be floored.

Add a couple of inches to all outside dimensions of the sheet(s) . . . you'll cut off the extra during installation. Trim off the excess and cut out any jogs with a sharp linoleum knife or a pair of heavy shears (see top sketch).If necessary, use a contour gauge to transfer intricate cutouts. Make circular cutouts for pipes, radiator legs, or other obstructions.

Installation

Remove any tape holding a seam in the vinyl and roll up the sheet so that the starter edge is on the outside. Carry the roll into the room to be floored. Align the edge with the starter wall and unroll the

sheet (see bottom sketch), allowing edges to roll up the wall on all four sides.

If you're working with two sheets that have to be seamed, roll out one and use the guidelines you drew to match up the second one. When pattern matches, squeeze the overlapping sheets together as tightly as possible (get a helper to stand on the seam) and cut through both pieces of vinyl, using a sharp knife and a straightedge. Remove the excess. Fold back both sheets to expose five or six inches of subflooring; then, spread a strip of seaming cement with a notched trowel. Butt edges neatly and press both sheets to the mastic.

Finish fitting the vinyl by trimming off the excess edges around the walls, leaving a ⅛-inch space between the floor and the wall. Slit the flooring between the wall edge and any cutouts.

When vinyl is completely in place and trimmed correctly, turn back the border and spray a special adhesive onto the subfloor (if desired). Flatten vinyl to floor; replace shoe molding.

HOW TO LAY CARPETING

Cushion-Backed Carpeting

Cushion-backed carpeting is the quickest do-it-yourself floor covering of all because it offers one-step installation. Before laying it, all you need do is remove shoe molding and clean the floor. Then, loosely fit the carpeting onto the floor, running it slightly up the walls on all sides. Pull tight and trim off excess. (For straight cuts when trimming, mark a chalk line around the perimeter of the room.)

If your room is wider than 15 feet, you'll have to seam two sections of carpet. Use two rows of double-faced carpet tape where seams fall (see sketch).

Cushion-backed carpeting is non-skid; however, if desired, you can add carpet tape or adhesive around the borders.

Jute-Backed Carpeting

This type includes a separate pad you must install beneath the carpeting. First, loosely fit the carpeting onto the floor. Then, roll back half of it and install padding on floor, tacking it every foot or so about three inches from the wall to prevent movement. Repeat for other half of room.

About one foot in from each of two adjacent walls, temporarily tack the carpeting. On the opposite side of the room—working the length first and stretching the carpet toward the corners—tack carpeting permanently into position in the same way described above. Repeat for the remaining three sides of carpet, removing temporary tacking as you go. NOTE: You can rent a small carpet stretcher—sometimes called a kicker—to help pull the carpeting tight (see sketch).

When carpeting is in place, fold back the edge along each wall, working one wall at a time. Trim 1½ inches off padding along wall. Then, hem carpeting under so it just meets the wall, and tack the double layer every six inches around the perimeter of room. Replace molding.

HOW TO INSTALL A FIREPLACE

You can cheer up even the chilliest winter evening with the pleasure of a glowing fire in your brand-new, built-in fireplace. The construction is surprisingly simple when you purchase a prefabricated fireplace kit like the one shown here.

Planning the Project

Take time to lay out your plans on paper before buying any materials. If you have questions about the fireplace installation, your building supply dealer can help you solve them. Also check local building codes to see what installation requirements or restrictions exist.

Then, decide what type of fireplace you want and where you want to locate it. Check manufacturer's specifications on any unit before purchasing it . . . there may be limitations on how closely you can locate the firebox to combustible material.

Getting Started

Place the firebox where you want to build the fireplace. Then run a plumb line from the ceiling to the center of the flue-pipe opening at the top of the box. Mark this spot on the ceiling and draw a square large enough to allow for two inches of clearance around flue pipe.

Cut a hole in the ceiling, boxing in the opening with the same size lumber as the ceiling joists. Insert a firestop spacer into the opening.

Everytime you cut through a floor, ceiling, or roof, follow this procedure: 1) measure, 2) mark opening, 3) cut and box-in hole, 4) install a firestop spacer.

Install Flue Pipe

Stack insulated flue pipe sections up through the ceiling and roof openings. Make sure you extend the pipe at least two feet higher than any portion of the roof within 10 feet (this will prevent downdrafts, which force smoke back

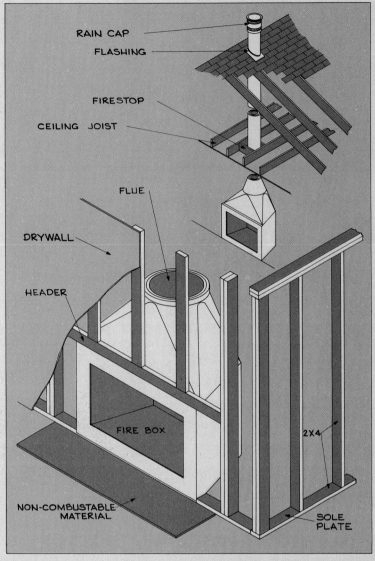

down through the flue pipe and into your room).

Close the roof opening as soon as possible. Fit flashing around the opening *exactly,* and use plenty of roofing tar. NOTE: As an option, you might want to run the flue pipe up the side of your house. Check manufacturer's specifications.

Framing the Firebox

Next, build a frame from 2x4s for the firebox. Measure and cut sole plates to size (see sketch) and anchor them to the floor with adhesive or nails.

Locate joists in the ceiling and drop a plumb line to mark location

of top plates. Position and nail 2x4 top plates onto the ceiling joists. Then, install studs in the arrangement that is shown in the sketch above (16 inches on center) also installing a 2x4 header over the firebox.

Facing the Framework

Cover the frame with plywood, particle board, or drywall. Then, choose a suitable facing material to set off the good looks of your new fireplace. Simulated brick or stone are good choices: they are attractive and easy to install.

Add a sheet of non-combustible material in front of fireplace for a hearth (see sketch).